Attention-Deficit/ Hyperactivity Disorder in Children and Adolescents

Attention-Deficit/ Hyperactivity Disorder in Children and Adolescents

A DSM-5 Handbook for Medical and Mental Health Professionals

Gordon Teichner

MP MOMENTUM PRESS
HEALTH

MOMENTUM PRESS, LLC, NEW YORK

Attention-Deficit/Hyperactivity Disorder in Children and Adolescents:
A DSM-5 Handbook for Medical and Mental Health Professionals

First published in 2017 by
Momentum Press, LLC
222 East 46th Street, New York, NY 10017
www.momentumpress.net

ISBN-13: 978-1-94474-935-4 (paperback)
ISBN-13: 978-1-94474-936-1 (e-book)

Momentum Press Child Clinical Psychology "Nuts and Bolts"
Collection

Cover and interior design by Exeter Premedia Services Private Ltd.,
Chennai, India

First edition: 2017

10 9 8 7 6 5 4 3 2 1

Printed in the United States of America.

Attention-Deficit/ Hyperactivity Disorder in Children and Adolescents

A DSM-5 Handbook for Medical and Mental Health Professionals

Gordon Teichner

MP MOMENTUM PRESS
HEALTH

MOMENTUM PRESS, LLC, NEW YORK

Attention-Deficit/Hyperactivity Disorder in Children and Adolescents:
A DSM-5 Handbook for Medical and Mental Health Professionals

First published in 2017 by
Momentum Press, LLC
222 East 46th Street, New York, NY 10017
www.momentumpress.net

ISBN-13: 978-1-94474-935-4 (paperback)
ISBN-13: 978-1-94474-936-1 (e-book)

Momentum Press Child Clinical Psychology "Nuts and Bolts"
Collection

Cover and interior design by Exeter Premedia Services Private Ltd.,
Chennai, India

First edition: 2017

10 9 8 7 6 5 4 3 2 1

Printed in the United States of America.

Abstract

Medical and mental health professionals who treat children and adolescents are frequently asked to evaluate and treat an Attention-Deficit/ Hyperactivity Disorder (ADHD). This can be a daunting task given a range of complex issues. This book presents valuable information that will assist professionals in this process. This handbook will be of benefit to physicians, physician assistants, nurse practitioners, psychologists, psychiatrists, mental health counselors, social workers, teachers, and graduate students. The reader will learn about the causes of ADHD, how to accurately diagnose ADHD, and methods to evaluate potential coexisting disorders that often accompany this condition. Professionals reading this book will gain a thorough understanding of empirically based treatments that work for ADHD. A number of case studies illustrating the assessment and treatment of ADHD are presented. The information presented in this handbook will offer professionals information that will benefit their patients who demonstrate ADHD. Mental health professionals who are looking to increase their revenue will also be interested in this book given the growing need for qualified providers who can provide assessment and treatment services for this population.

Keywords

ADHD, adolescents, attention-deficit/hyperactivity disorder, behavior modification, behavior therapy, behavioral parent training, children, comorbidity, developmental, learning disorders, medication, neuropsychological assessment, pediatric, pharmacotherapy, psychological assessment, treatment

Contents

Acknowledgments

I would like to thank my family, friends, staff, and colleagues who have supported me throughout the process of this publication. I am particularly grateful to Paul Robbins, MD; Randy Waid, PhD; and Jeff Selman, PsyD, who graciously reviewed drafts of this book. Guys, your feedback was invaluable, and your friendships are very important to me.

To my wife Sonja whom I love and cherish. Thank you for helping me throughout this journey. I am a much better man with you in my life.

Finally, I am eternally thankful to all of the children, adolescents, and adults with ADHD that I have evaluated and treated over the years. It has been a privilege to serve you. I hope that I have been able to help you improve the quality of your lives and succeed in your endeavors.

CHAPTER 1

Description and Diagnosis of Attention-Deficit/ Hyperactivity Disorder

DSM-5 Diagnostic Criteria for Attention-Deficit/ Hyperactivity Disorder

Attention-Deficit/Hyperactivity Disorder (ADHD) is a neurodevelopmental disorder that is characterized by symptoms of inattention, impulsivity, and hyperactivity that are inconsistent with a child's developmental level. Several symptoms must be displayed across two or more settings. Difficulties associated with ADHD must significantly interfere with, or reduce the quality of, the child's functioning (e.g., at home, at school, in academic performance, in leisure activities, in relations with others, in managing daily responsibilities) in order to meet the criteria for this diagnosis.

Symptom onset has been changed in DSM-5 (American Psychiatric Association, 2013) to prior to the age of 12 years; several symptoms of inattention, hyperactivity, and impulsivity must have been present prior to this age in order to meet the DSM-5 diagnostic criteria. DSM-IV (American Psychiatric Association, 1994) and DSM-IV-TR (American Psychiatric Association, 2000) definitions required a symptom onset prior to the age of seven years in order to meet diagnostic criteria for ADHD.

ADHD is a neurodevelopmental condition that can result in a range of functional difficulties for the child. Males and females generally display equal levels of persistent academic, behavioral, and social problems (Hinshaw et al., 2012). Such difficulties may include academic underachievement, learning disorders, externalizing behavior problems, psychological difficulties, problems with peer relations, and substance usage. Such issues often precipitate a referral to evaluating and treating clinicians.

DSM-5 indicates that the prevalence of ADHD in children is about 5 percent across cultures. ADHD is more frequently demonstrated by boys, with a ratio of approximately 2:1 in children. Girls are more likely to primarily demonstrate symptoms comprising the ADHD symptom cluster of Inattention.

Listed in the following are the DSM-5 diagnostic criteria for ADHD (American Psychiatric Association, 2013).

Attention-Deficit/Hyperactivity Disorder—DSM-5 Diagnostic Criteria

A. A persistent pattern of inattention and/or hyperactivity-impulsivity that interferes with functioning or development, as characterized by (1) and/or (2):

1. **Inattention:** Six (or more) of the following symptoms have persisted for at least six months to a degree that is inconsistent with developmental level and that negatively impacts directly on social and academic/occupational activities:

    Note: The symptoms are not solely a manifestation of oppositional behavior, defiance, hostility, or failure to understand tasks or instructions. For older adolescents and adults (age 17 years and older), at least five symptoms must be present.

    a. Often fails to give close attention to details or makes careless mistakes in schoolwork, at work, or during other activities (e.g., overlooks or misses details; work is inaccurate).

    b. Often has difficulty sustaining attention in tasks or play activities (e.g., has difficulty remaining focused during lectures, conversations, or lengthy reading).

    c. Often does not seem to listen when spoken to directly (e.g., mind seems elsewhere, even in the absence of any obvious distraction).

    d. Often does not follow through on instructions and fails to finish schoolwork, chores, or duties in the workplace (e.g., starts tasks but quickly loses focus and is easily sidetracked).

    e. Often has difficulty organizing tasks and activities (e.g., difficulty managing sequential tasks; difficulty keeping materials and belongings in order; messy, disorganized work; has poor time management; fails to meet deadlines).

f. Often avoids, dislikes, or is reluctant to engage in tasks that require sustained mental effort (e.g., schoolwork or homework; for older adolescents and adults, preparing reports, completing forms, reviewing lengthy papers).

g. Often loses things necessary for tasks or activities (e.g., school materials, pencils, books, tools, wallet, keys, paperwork, eyeglasses, mobile phone).

h. Is often easily distracted by extraneous stimuli (for older adolescents and adults, this may include unrelated thoughts).

i. Is often forgetful in daily activities (e.g., doing chores, running errands; for older adolescents and adults, returning calls, paying bills, keeping appointments).

2. **Hyperactivity and Impulsivity:** Six (or more) of the following symptoms have persisted for at least six months to a degree that is inconsistent with developmental level and that negatively impacts directly on social and academic/occupational activities:

   Note: The symptoms are not solely a manifestation of oppositional behavior, defiance, hostility, or a failure to understand tasks or instructions. For older adolescents and adults (age 17 years and older), at least five symptoms must be present.

   a. Often fidgets with or taps hands or feet or squirms in seat.

   b. Often leaves seat in situations when remaining seated is expected (e.g., leaves his or her place in the classroom, in the office or workplace, or in other situations that require remaining in place).

   c. Often runs about or climbs in situations where it is inappropriate. (In adolescents or adults, this may be limited to feeling restless).

   d. Often unable to play or engage in leisure activities quietly.

   e. Is often "on the go," acting as if "driven by a motor" (e.g., is unable to be or is uncomfortable being still for extended time, as in restaurants, meetings; the child may be experienced by others as being restless or difficult to keep up with).

   f. Often talks excessively.

g. Often blurts out an answer before a question has been completed (e.g., completes people's sentences; cannot wait for turn
in conversation).

h. Often has difficulty waiting his or her turn (e.g., while waiting
in line).

i. Often interrupts or intrudes on others (e.g., interrupts conversations, games, or activities; may start using other people's
things without asking or receiving permission; for adolescents
and adults, may intrude into or take over what others are
doing).

B. Several inattentive or hyperactive-impulsive symptoms were present
prior to age 12 years.

C. Several inattentive or hyperactive-impulsive symptoms are present
in two or more settings (e.g., at home, at school, or at work; with
friends or relatives; in other activities).

D. There is clear evidence that the symptoms interfere with, or reduce
the quality of, social, academic/occupational functioning.

E. The symptoms do not occur exclusively during the course of schizophrenia or another psychotic disorder and are not better explained
by another mental disorder (e.g., mood disorder, anxiety disorder,
dissociative disorder, personality disorder, substance intoxication or
withdrawal).

Specify Whether

1. **314.01 (F90.2) Combined presentation:** If both Criterion A1
(Inattention) and Criterion A2 (Hyperactivity-Impulsivity) are met
for the past six months.

2. **314.00 (F90.0) Predominantly inattentive presentation:** If
Criterion A1 (Inattention) is met but Criterion A2 (Hyperactivity-
Impulsivity) is not met for the past six months.

3. **314.01 (F90.1) Predominantly hyperactive/impulsive presentation:** If Criterion A2 (Hyperactivity-Impulsivity) is met and
Criterion A1 (Inattention) is not met for the past six months.

4. **314.01 (F90.8) Other Specified Attention-Deficit/Hyperactivity
Disorder:** This category applies to presentations in which symptoms

characteristic of ADHD that cause significant distress or impairment in social, occupational, or other important areas of functioning predominate but do not meet the full criteria for ADHD or any of the disorders in the neurodevelopmental disorders diagnostic class. The Other Specified ADHD category is used in situations in which the clinician chooses to communicate the specific reason for the presentation not meeting the criteria for ADHD or any specific neurodevelopmental disorder. This is done by recording "Other Specified Attention-deficit/hyperactivity Disorder" followed by the specific reason (e.g., "with insufficient inattentive symptoms").

5. **314.01   (F90.9)   Unspecified   Attention-Deficit/Hyperactivity Disorder:** This category applies to presentations in which symptoms characteristic of ADHD that cause clinically significant distress or impairment in social, occupational, or other important areas of functioning predominate but do not meet the full criteria for ADHD or any of the disorders in the neurodevelopmental disorders diagnostic class. The Unspecified ADHD category is used in situations in which the clinician chooses not to specify the reason the criteria are not met for ADHD or for a specific neurodevelopmental disorder, and includes presentations in which there is insufficient information to make a more specific diagnosis.

Specify Whether

1. **In partial remission:** When full criteria were previously met, fewer than the full criteria have been met for the past six months, and the symptoms still result in impairment in social, academic/occupational functioning.

Specify Current Severity

1. **Mild:** Few, if any, symptoms in excess of those required to make the diagnosis are present, and symptoms result in no more than minor impairments in social or occupational functioning.
2. **Moderate:** Symptoms or functional impairment between "mild" and "severe" are present.

3. **Severe:** Many symptoms in excess of those required to make the diagnosis, or several symptoms that are particularly severe, are present, or the symptoms result in marked impairment in social or occupational functioning.

Executive Dysfunction

ADHD is a neurobiological disorder that is characterized by executive deficits. In many ways, ADHD can be conceptualized as a spectrum disorder in the sense that its symptom presentation can differ greatly between individuals. The aforementioned symptoms of inattention, hyperactivity, and impulsivity comprise the core features of ADHD. However, it is common for many children and adolescents with ADHD to display a range of additional frontal systems challenges that can negatively impact their functioning.

ADHD is a biologically based condition that is primarily due to deficits associated with the frontal lobe and related frontal systems. The prefrontal cortex of the brain and its various neural pathways to different brain structures are involved in a range of neurocognitive and neurobehavioral functions over and above attention/concentration, activity level, and control on one's impulses. These functions are known as executive abilities. Executive skills include planning, organization, applying logic, reasoning, problem solving, behavioral initiation, motivation, persistence, delaying gratification, information processing speed, self-management of time, judgment, insight, cognitive flexibility, and regulating one's emotions. Children and adolescents with ADHD may potentially demonstrate some combination of such executive difficulties over and above symptoms of inattention, hyperactivity, and impulsivity. An understanding of such challenges can often be important in guiding specific interventions targeting specific areas of concern.

Differential Diagnosis

ADHD is somewhat of a complex neurodevelopmental disorder to assess when considering that some of its symptoms and behaviors may be a function of a competing condition and not ADHD itself. The evaluative process needs to take into consideration a range of other psychological, neurodevelopmental, and substance use disorders when determining if the child truly demonstrates ADHD, or if symptoms are better accounted for by an alternate condition.

Common rule-out diagnoses in the differential diagnosis process include Behavioral Disorders (e.g., Oppositional Defiant Disorder, Conduct Disorder), Anxiety Disorders (e.g., Generalized Anxiety Disorder), Mood Disorders (e.g., Major Depressive Disorder, Persistent Depressive Disorders, Bipolar Disorder, Disruptive Mood Dysregulation Disorder), Neurodevelopmental Disorders (e.g., Autism Spectrum Disorder, Tourette's Disorder, Intellectual Disability), Reactive Attachment Disorder, Substance Use Disorders, Psychotic Disorders, and Specific Learning Disorders.

Comorbidity

Making matters more difficult is the fact that many children and adolescents with ADHD demonstrate comorbid DSM-5 disorders. ADHD is a condition where comorbidity is the rule rather than exception. It is estimated that at least 80 percent of children with ADHD concurrently display one or more comorbid disorders (Willcutt & Bidwell, 2011). Any of the aforementioned behavioral, psychological, substance use, learning, or neurodevelopmental conditions may accompany an ADHD diagnosis. An understanding of the gestalt of the child is paramount so that all pertinent issues can be appropriately addressed.

Precise comorbidity estimates in regard to how frequently specific disorders are demonstrated in conjunction with ADHD are difficult to determine given that results vary across studies. Willcutt and Bidwell (2011) reviewed the literature indicating a relatively high frequency of comorbid disorders that often accompany ADHD. For example, Oppositional Defiant Disorder is present for approximately 30 to 60 percent of children with ADHD, with close to 50 percent of children with the Combined Presentation of ADHD concurrently displaying this behavioral disorder. A more serious Conduct Disorder is displayed by 20 to 50 percent of children with ADHD Combined Presentation. Other conditions such as anxiety disorders (15 to 30 percent) and depressive disorders (15 to

30 percent) are common. Approximately 10 percent of children with ADHD have a tic disorder (MTA Cooperative Group, 1999), although 50 to 60 percent of children with tic disorders have ADHD (Rothenberger, Roessner, Banashewki, & Leckman, 2007). The prevalence rates of children with intellectual disabilities and comorbid ADHD are 18 to 40 percent, while children with Autism Spectrum Disorders demonstrate comorbid ADHD at rates of 18 to 40 percent (Murray, 2010). Disruptive Mood Dysregulation Disorder is a new condition that has been introduced into DSM-5. The majority of children and adolescents with a Disruptive Mood Dysregulation Disorder concurrently display ADHD. However, the prevalence of a Disruptive Mood Dysregulation Disorder among children and adolescents is estimated to fall in the 2 to 5 percent range (American Psychiatric Association, 2013). In reality only a smaller percentage of children and adolescents demonstrating ADHD concurrently display a Disruptive Mood Dysregulation Disorder.

Research indicates that children with ADHD are more likely to display a comorbid Specific Learning Disorder compared with their peers. A recent literature review by DuPaul, Gormley, and Larracy (2013) concluded that the comorbidity rate is as high as 45 percent. Further, it is not uncommon for children with ADHD to underachieve academically, receive poor grades, or be less productive compared with their peers. DuPaul and Stoner (2014) estimate that learning and/or academic achievement problems are prevalent for 50 to 80 percent of samples of children and adolescents with ADHD.

It is important for the evaluating psychologist, psychiatrist, or physician to perform a thorough exam when assessing for ADHD given this potentially complex differential picture and high comorbidity rates that accompany this condition. It is not uncommon for many children with ADHD to continue to struggle academically, psychologically, and/or socially even after ADHD has been correctly identified and treated. This is sometimes due to the fact that comorbid conditions have gone undiagnosed and untreated.

Not every child or adolescent with potential ADHD needs to undergo a comprehensive evaluation via a psychologist or psychiatrist. Many pediatricians and other family physicians are fully competent in identifying ADHD. Again, such providers should be cognizant of this high comorbidity rate for children and adolescents who demonstrate ADHD. At minimum such potential concerns should be screened via some sort of objective screening method. The possibility of comorbidity should also be considered if the child does not respond as expected to reasonable treatment efforts, displays unusual or negative responses to treatments, or if functional difficulties (e.g., academic impairments, impaired social relationships) persist. A referral to a psychologist or psychiatrist for a comprehensive evaluation may be warranted in such cases. Such a referral is also appropriate when comorbidity is suspected but such issues are beyond the scope of practice of the treating professional.

Other Issues to Consider When Evaluating for ADHD

Several other issues are important to consider when determining if a child or adolescent does or does not demonstrate ADHD:

1. **ADHD reflects a *persistent* pattern of symptoms (i.e., inattention and/or hyperactivity-impulsivity).**
   Symptoms of ADHD are typically ongoing and continuous. Symptoms do not suddenly emerge and remit over time. The child who displays this condition is typically born with a biological predisposition to manifest this condition. Symptoms may gradually emerge around a specific age. In many cases, longer-standing symptoms become more apparent at certain ages given resultant functional difficulties (e.g., academic problems, with one's social interactions, managing one's day-to-day activities). As such, it is important for the examining clinician to understand the course of potential ADHD-related symptoms.

   Some clinicians may differ with this perspective and point out that a range of acquired brain insults (e.g., traumatic brain injury) can result in ADHD. As such, there may be an acute onset of symptoms and the course may not necessarily be continuous. Others may opine that some medical conditions (e.g., epilepsy) can result in ADHD. Children with such neurologically based challenges may certainly display symptoms that appear to meet DSM-5 diagnostic criteria for ADHD. It is often important to differentiate an "acquired" ADHD from the more common developmentally based ADHD. Children with such neurologically based conditions often present with additional, qualitatively different symptoms compared with children with a developmentally based ADHD. Comorbid conditions and other neurocognitive challenges may be present. Such children sometimes do not respond to pharmacological interventions in the typical fashion that children with a developmentally based ADHD will. Neuropsychological testing is often helpful when examining such children, including in the process of guiding recommendations for treatment and educational planning.

Making matters more complex in some children is the possibility that variants of both acquired and developmentally based ADHD may be simultaneously present. For example, a child may demonstrate a true developmentally based Attention-Deficit/Hyperactivity Disorder. However, some of their symptoms and/or the severity of their symptoms may be caused or exacerbated by other variables. Such may be the case in a traumatic brain injury. These children in particular may benefit from objective neuropsychological assessment rather than the clinician relying only on behavior checklists, history, and clinical interviews.

2. **ADHD begins in childhood.**

Research indicates that symptoms of ADHD emerge prior to the age of 12 years. Several symptoms of inattention, hyperactivity, or impulsivity must have been displayed in childhood (i.e., prior to the age of 12 years) in order to possibly meet diagnostic criteria for this condition. A person does not demonstrate ADHD if symptoms began at a different time (e.g., late adolescence, adulthood). The clinician must consider a different etiology accounting for an individual's symptom complaints if such symptoms truly began after childhood. As such, it is very important that the evaluating clinician establishes the age at which symptoms first began to occur. In this process, it is also important to understand what specific symptoms were present during childhood. Understanding the developmental course of such symptoms is especially important when evaluating adolescents and adults for ADHD given that presenting symptom complaints could be due to a competing condition and not ADHD.

This criterion reflects one of the major changes made in the DSM-5 diagnostic criteria of ADHD compared with criteria specified in DSM-IV (American Psychiatric Association, 1994) and DSM-IV-TR (American Psychiatric Association, 2000). These prior versions of the DSM maintained that symptoms must have been present prior to the age of seven years. A decision was made to change this criterion to prior to the age of 12 years in the DSM-5 given research findings indicating that this age criterion is more accurate.

3. **Symptoms of ADHD must be displayed in more than one setting.** One of the issues to consider in making a diagnosis of ADHD is that symptoms must be displayed in more than one setting (e.g., at home, in the classroom, in after-school programs, during activities, while playing sports, during social interactions). The evaluating clinician must ensure that ADHD-related symptoms are truly displayed in two or more settings, and are not solely specific to a certain location or activity.

ADHD is a biologically based condition. Not surprisingly, symptoms of true ADHD are typically demonstrated across settings. Children with ADHD often exhibit symptoms of inattention, hyperactivity, or impulsivity at home, at school, with friends, during activities, and in other aspects of their daily lives.

It is sometimes difficult to understand the variety of settings where such symptoms are displayed by the child. This may be due to the fact that the actual manifestation and functional impact of ADHD-related symptoms can vary depending on a range of factors such as the age of the child, severity of symptoms, presence of comorbid conditions, demands of the task, or factors specific to the setting itself. This could also be due to limitations in the quality or accuracy of reporting as offered by the parent or child.

For example, ADHD-related symptoms may be minimal if the child is receiving one-to-one tutoring, if the child is engaged in academic tasks that they find interesting, when the child is playing video games, or when they are offered close supervision. Symptoms may be evident and problematic in a number of other contexts such as when engaged in independent study, when in a large classroom of children, when performing academic tasks that are not of interest, when engaging in boring or repetitive tasks, or when direct supervision is unavailable.

4. **Symptoms of ADHD must interfere with, or reduce the quality of, social, academic/occupational functioning.**

   ADHD typically results in functional difficulties or impairments. To meet DSM-5 diagnostic criteria, symptoms must interfere with, or reduce the quality of, functioning in a range of life's activities. It is important for the evaluating clinician to determine how ADHD-related symptoms have potentially caused functional difficulties or impairments for the child who is being evaluated.

   For example, symptoms of inattention may negatively impact academic functioning. This could be displayed in poor grades, academic underachievement, requiring excessive parental oversight, or academic tasks taking much longer than they should. The child may not efficiently encode presented information given difficulties with sustained attention. Inattention (e.g., poor sustained attention, inattention to details) may negatively impact test taking, assignments, and homework. Other inattentive symptoms (e.g., disorganization, losing homework) may result in similar negative outcomes.

   Inattentive symptoms of ADHD may negatively impact the child's functioning at home (e.g., wandering off task; not following through with tasks; parents having to retrieve books from school that the child forgot to bring home), in sports (e.g., not following directions; forgetting plays; not appropriately attending to the game itself), in other activities, in interactions with peers, or in managing other daily responsibilities. Inattention symptoms may also negatively impact adolescents' operation of a motor vehicle.

   Symptoms of hyperactivity may negatively impact the child's or adolescent's functioning. For example, excessive talking may land them in trouble at school. Such behavior may be viewed negatively by friends and peers. Symptoms of hyperactivity may make it difficult for the child to remain seated for an extended period of time. This may negatively affect their ability to complete necessary academic work. Their restlessness, fidgeting, and out of seat behavior may possibly negatively impact their academic performance, social activities, social interactions with peers, time management, and completion of tasks as required.

Symptoms of impulsivity may have a negative impact on the individual's functioning in a number of different contexts. For example, uncontrolled impulsivity may negatively impact the child's functioning in school, at home, or with peers. Such uncontrolled impulsivity may manifest in blurting, not thinking before speaking, interrupting others, intruding on others' activities, or attempting to take over others' activities. Such behavior is often negatively viewed by peers and adults alike. Uncontrolled impulsivity is also demonstrated in poor emotional control by some children with ADHD. This may be expressed in temper tantrums, anger, acting-out behaviors, aggression, or other manifestations of emotional dyscontrol. Such behavior can negatively impact the child's functioning at school, at home, in leisure activities, with peers, and in other contexts.

Understanding the Clinical Presentation of Attention-Deficit/Hyperactivity Disorder

It is important to have a thorough understanding of DSM-5 criteria when assessing for a potential Attention-Deficit/Hyperactivity Disorder in children and adolescents. This includes detailed knowledge of how each symptom can manifest in day-to-day behavior. The following is a brief discussion of how specific DSM-5 ADHD criterion may be behaviorally displayed by children and adolescents. A number of clinical examples are offered to illustrate each symptom.

Inattention Symptoms

1. *Often fails to give close attention to details or makes careless mistakes in schoolwork, at work, or during other activities.*

   Many children with ADHD make careless errors in their schoolwork. They may rush through tests, assignments, and other academic tasks. It is common for such children to not read directions carefully. They may miss important details in their work. Such children may copy information incorrectly (e.g., in relation to assignments, due dates, directions). They may not read all parts of test questions. Children with ADHD may not answer some test or assignment questions due to inattention. Sometimes they may miss entire sections or fail to complete questions on the other side of the page. The child may not put their name on their work. They generally have trouble with tasks that require attention to details. Teachers, parents, tutors, and others may comment that the child struggles to pay close attention to details. Comments may be offered by others that the student often makes careless mistakes in his or her work.

Some academic subjects (e.g., math) especially require close attention to details. Failure to do so may result in incorrect calculations and errors. Children with ADHD may not pay attention to the operations sign (e.g., +, –). They may not line up columns neatly, leading to careless mistakes. They may omit steps in calculations. Decimal points may be placed incorrectly.

As a child grows older, the onus to complete various types of paperwork increasingly becomes his or her responsibility. This may include various school forms, job applications, college applications, and so forth. Inattention to details may plague such older adolescents, leading to careless errors. They may not answer all questions, fail to provide all necessary information, or make a range of other careless mistakes.

Example: Bradley is a 9-year-old boy who has not been doing well academically. He likes to be one of the first students to complete a test. His teacher has commented that he appears to rush through his exams. She has reported that he frequently makes careless errors on exams and assignments. Bradley's teacher adds that she has often sent him back to his seat to complete work that he has handed in because he frequently forgets to answer a number of questions. There have been times where Bradley has left blank the other side of the page where additional questions are listed. Careless errors have especially hurt his performance in math. Some of his math answers have been wrong because he has added when he should have subtracted and vice versa. He sometimes puts decimals in the wrong place. Bradley's mother reviews his homework with him nightly. She reports that she almost always has to draw his attention to a number of careless errors that he has made in his work.

2. *Often has difficulty sustaining attention in tasks or play activities.*
Many of life's activities require us to stay focused for extended periods of time. Such capacity is paramount in the learning process. Children who struggle with sustained attention often have difficulty staying focused during their classes. They may miss important information, concepts, instructions, and so forth given such difficulties. Such children may describe that they often drift off in their thoughts. They may think about extraneous information that is not relevant to the class lesson or task at hand. This equally affects many children when they are engaged in study or other assignment completion. Many children describe that they often have to reread information in order to gain comprehension and retention. This may be due to difficulty sustaining their attention throughout the reading task. This may result in encoding difficulties. The information read is not efficiently encoded to memory. Thus, the child may not be able to recall what they read, or recall important details from the text, because the information was not encoded to memory due to inattention. Further, such children and adolescents may have problems sustaining their attention in tasks that they may find boring, repetitive, or unstimulating.

Other life tasks require the capacity to sustain one's attention for extended periods of time. These include receiving directions or instructions from others. Holding conversations with others require us to maintain our focus for a period of time. Difficulties with sustained attention can also affect the child in sports or other structured activities where such capacity is important. This may also be a problem for older adolescents who hold a part-time job. Such youth may struggle to sustain their attention in tasks that require such abilities. In turn, this can result in poor work performance, inefficiency absorbing conveyed information, or other errors.

Example: Sarah is a bright 16-year-old who reports difficulty sustaining her attention in a range of tasks. She notes that she does not have much trouble staying focused on academic subjects that she enjoys, although she adds that she really only enjoys English,

Drama, and Art. However, engaging in subject areas that she finds boring is very challenging. She says that it is especially hard for her to sustain her attention in her Algebra and Science classes. She indicated that she consistently finds her mind drifting in these classes. Sarah acknowledges that she has always found Math and Science to be tedious and boring. She has never experienced any reading delays. Nonetheless, she reports that she often has to reread things in order to gain comprehension and retention, and this is more so for reading tasks that do not interest her. She indicates that she understands the taught math concepts. However, it often takes her minimally twice the amount of time to complete math worksheets and homework compared with her friends, as she struggles to stay focused on the problems. She states that it also takes her a long time to complete academic tasks that she enjoys. Sarah adds that she runs out of time on perhaps 30 percent of timed exams. She is often rushed on other tests and quizzes. She states that it is not uncommon for her mind to wander during tests. Sarah just started a part-time job as a hostess at a restaurant. Her direct supervisor has told her several times that she needs to pay better attention to instructions. She has made frequent errors because she has forgotten some of the directions given to her. Sarah's friends have also become upset with her at times. She states that several have commented, "...don't you remember we talked about that?" A few have expressed that this has hurt their feelings. They have commented that perhaps Sarah does not really care about them and what they have to say. Sarah says that this is not true—she cares about her friends, and states that on occasion she honestly does not remember some details of what they had discussed.

3. *Often does not seem to listen when spoken to directly (e.g., mind seems elsewhere, even in the absence of any obvious distraction).*
   One could become rich in a relatively short amount of time if children and adolescents with ADHD were charged money for every time they said "what?" or "huh?" Children with this symptom often struggle to encode information presented verbally. This is typically due to inattention, and not auditory comprehension (i.e., stemming from an auditory processing disorder), albeit it is possible to have both challenges. Such children often appear to be drifting in

their thoughts or thinking about other things when they are spoken to directly. A percentage recognize that they missed aspects of the conveyed information. In turn, they may ask questions or ask the speaker to repeat the information. Adults who are familiar with the child (e.g., parents, teachers) may recognize that the child was not listening. As such, they may often repeat instructions, directions, and other important information. It is often apparent that the child was not listening when the other person asks them to repeat the information and they cannot do so.

It is important to consider some factors in determining if this symptom is truly present. Of primary concern is volitional behavior. Some children purposely ignore others, including what the speaker is saying. Such behavior reflects a very different phenomenon and should not be considered a reflection of this ADHD-related symptom. Taking environmental variables into consideration is also important. For example, a child who often does not seem to be listening when spoken to directly *only* in situations where multiple external distractors are present would not meet the criteria for this symptom.

Example: Omar is an 8-year-old boy who is presenting for clinical exam. His father states that he constantly has to repeat things to Omar even when he appears to have his full attention. Omar claims that he often forgets what was said. His father indicates that Omar is not a defiant child; he legitimately seems to not remember instructions and directions. More recently, Omar's father has routinely had him immediately repeat instructions and other important information. He comments that Omar seems to be able to repeat the information correctly less than 50 percent of the time. He often has to have Omar repeat what was said two or three times to be confident that he truly heard and understood what was said. Omar's teacher at school has raised similar concerns. She says that Omar always indicates that he understands the instructions and he never has any questions. It is then common for him to ask questions only a few minutes later about what was just discussed. At other times, she has to repeat directions and prompt him to start working because he clearly does not know what to do. This has been the case even though instructions were just given a few minutes prior. Omar's teacher comments that he appears eager to learn, and he never displays any disruptive classroom behavior. She feels that this inattention does not appear to reflect volitional behavior.

4. *Often does not follow through on instructions and fails to finish school-work, chores, or duties in the workplace.*

Children with ADHD often struggle to complete a range of different tasks. It is not uncommon that they may start yet not finish tasks. Such children can often lose focus or become easily sidetracked by other things. This can negatively impact their academic performance, given that they may not finish necessary assignments or homework. Such behavior can also negatively impact studying. The child may go from task to task and not encode the information efficiently.

Children with ADHD often do not follow through on instructions. Multistep instructions can be especially problematic. They may become easily sidetracked and not complete tasks that they were instructed to do. Such behavior may relate to chores, hygiene tasks, homework, or other day-to-day responsibilities.

Such challenges are often displayed by older adolescents who hold a part-time job. They may struggle to follow through on instructions or complete necessary tasks, and may inefficiently go from task to task. Such behavior can obviously negatively impact their work performance.

It is important to consider the potential voluntary display of such behavior by some children and adolescents when considering if this symptom is truly demonstrated. Refusal to follow instructions does not constitute this symptom. Equally, a purposeful decision by the child to simply not complete schoolwork, chores, or other tasks reflects a different behavioral phenomenon.

Example: Jose is a 13-year-old boy whose parents decided to bring him to counseling because of his poor academic grades. Jose qualified for the school district's "Gifted and Talented Program" during elementary school. Jose did well academically through most of elementary school, but his grades have progressively declined since the fifth grade. His grades have been especially poor this academic year.

Jose states that he never answers test questions in order. He prefers to skip around. He offers several examples illustrating how he lost points because he inadvertently did not complete some test sections and questions. He says that he has also lost points on math worksheets and tests for not showing his work. Jose comments that he does not feel that this is fair as he knows how to do the work and writing out all of the steps is not necessary. Inspection of his academic records reveals multiple poor homework grades including many where he received a zero as the assignment was not completed. Jose acknowledges that he often does not complete homework. At other times he may start homework but becomes bored or sidetracked, goes on to another task, and never completes the assignment in its entirety. Jose's mother reports that if she wants him to complete a task (e.g., a chore), she needs to communicate to him the specific instruction for a single task, wait for him to finish, and then assign the next task as needed. She comments that he will likely become distracted and not complete all assigned tasks if she were to give him instructions that involve several steps (e.g., put away your clothes, come back and empty the dishwater, then take out the garbage). Jose's mother says that he has been this way since very early childhood.

5. *Often has difficulty organizing tasks and activities.*

Good organization is important to academic success. Children with ADHD are often poorly organized. They struggle to organize various aspects of their schoolwork such as necessary homework, assignments, test dates, and due dates. Their binders and book bags may be exceptionally messy and disorganized. Such children have difficulty keeping their materials together in an organized fashion. Their note taking, assignments, and other academic work may be disorganized as well. Children with ADHD may struggle to put necessary information in proper, ordered steps. They often struggle with sequential information. Difficulties with organization may also be reflected in poor prioritization of various tasks. Such children often struggle with time management. They are often poor at planning, tend to procrastinate, and may turn in necessary work late. Children who struggle with poor organization often require deadlines and consequences to complete a range of tasks.

Poor organization can also negatively impact the child's functioning in other activities. This may include not having all necessary items when participating in sports, scouts, groups, or other recreational activities.

Many parents often recognize that their child is poorly organized. It is not uncommon for parents to assist their child in an attempt to help the child compensate for this behavior. They may take steps to organize their child. Some take over most aspects of organization given the severity of the problem. It is often helpful for the evaluating clinician to ask parents if they have taken the onus of organizing their child when determining if the child truly displays this symptom.

Example: Lamar is a 10-year-old boy who reportedly struggles with organization. His parents indicate that such poor organization has negatively impacted his academic performance, and has also negatively affected him in other tasks. Teachers have repeatedly offered feedback since the first grade that his desk is very disorganized. It has been such a problem that Lamar frequently cannot find materials that he needs. Teachers have also reported that his work is often messy and disorganized. Lamar reports that his binders are disorganized. He says that his book bag usually looks like "...something exploded in it." He reports that his parents often tell him that his bedroom looks like a tornado just went through. Lamar's mother indicates that she has always helped him to pack his school bag, organize his binders, and so forth, and has set up various organizational systems over the years. She reports that she recently made the decision to let him try to organize himself. She thought that suffering natural consequences for poor organization may help him to change his behavior. This apparently was a disaster. For example, Lamar's Scout Troop leader recently contacted her after the fact that he did not bring enough clothes and he forgot several important pieces of equipment that were needed for a recent overnight scouting trip. His football coach has called his parents several times because Lamar has forgotten to bring all of his equipment to several practice sessions. Lamar's parents also note a significant decline in grades since they began letting him organize himself. Several assignments have not been completed. Multiple homework assignments were never completed, while others that were completed were never handed in. Lamar claims that he never purposely chose not to do those assignments and homework. He says that he planned to do them but then ran out of time. For others, he states that he completed the homework but was unable to find it when it was necessary to turn it in. His mother reports that she later found several homework assignments buried in his book bag and in a stack of papers on the desk in his room.

6. *Often avoids, dislikes, or is reluctant to engage in tasks that require sustained mental effort.*

   Children and adolescents with ADHD often avoid and dislike tasks that require sustained mental effort. This often pertains to schoolwork and homework. Such children are often reluctant to engage in such tasks. They may put forth minimal effort in relation to the completion of assignments and homework. The amount of time studying may be minimal to none. Such children often procrastinate with assignments. Other tasks that are boring or repetitive may also be a struggle. Such behavior may be demonstrated especially in subject areas that the child does not find interesting (e.g., mathematics). Better effort is sometimes displayed in subject areas that they find interesting.

   For older adolescents, such behavior may also be demonstrated in procrastinating with completing necessary forms (e.g., a job application, college application), work tasks they may find boring or repetitive, and avoiding other tasks requiring sustained mental effort.

   Example: David is a 12-year-old boy who has always struggled academically. Over the years, teachers have frequently commented that he is not living up to his full academic potential. A good proportion of his poor grades appear to be the outcome of secondary to poor academic effort. David openly acknowledges that he does not like school. He says that he never studies. He may or may not complete homework. Minimal effort is offered when he does complete homework and other necessary assignments. David reports that he does just enough work to get by academically. He says that he does not care about getting good grades. It is fine as long as he passes. David indicates that he finds it very difficult to motivate himself to complete many academic tasks and assignments. He states that this is even more so for subject areas that he does not find interesting, such as math. His mother adds that he often procrastinates; he will literally wait until the last minute possible to complete various assignments, and he completes this work only due to her repeated prompting. David's mother states that poor motivation and effort are also demonstrated for other tasks that may be difficult or require sustained mental effort. Several examples were offered, such as his participation in different sports, Boy Scouts, the school newspaper, and various chores. David finds it difficult to motivate himself to do such tasks, and he often gives up easily if the task is difficult. Such behavior has been persistent since a young age.

7. *Often loses things necessary for tasks or activities* (e.g., school materials, pencils, books, tools, wallet, keys, paperwork, eyeglasses, mobile phone).

Children and adolescents with ADHD lose things on a regular basis. They often misplace their phone, keys, identification, wallet, glasses, and other items. They may spend a substantial amount of time looking for completed assignments that they placed somewhere in their book bag. Such children may also spend a considerable amount of time looking for toys, tools, school materials, clothes, and other items. The may frequently ask their parents where such items may possibly be located. It is not uncommon for such children to put down an item (e.g., phone, worksheet) and then not remember a few minutes later where they placed the item. Such children and adolescents often struggle with time management.

Example: La'Teisha is a 15-year-old girl who is referred for psychological assessment to rule out the possibility of an Attention-Deficit/ Hyperactivity Disorder. Both she and her mother report that she frequently loses things that she needs for her daily tasks and activities. La'Teisha says that she loses her cell phone, keys, and school ID multiple times daily. She often places such items and then cannot recall where she put things a short while later. She reports that she is constantly looking for clothes, homework, school books, school ID, keys, and other items. She notes that this is very frustrating because she usually spends a considerable amount of time each day looking for things that she cannot find. She adds that she has lost well in excess of 15 homework assignments this year. She insists that she completed this homework, yet was unable to remember what she had done with it when it was time to turn it in. She adds that she redid and handed in missed homework assignments as she is motivated to do well academically. Unfortunately, her teachers deducted some points given that the assignments were submitted late. La'Teisha reports that she found most of these lost assignments the next semester when she was cleaning out her book bag and bedroom.

8. *Is often easily distracted by extraneous stimuli* (for older adolescents and adults, this may include unrelated thoughts).

Children and adolescents with ADHD are often easily distracted by other things going on around them. A range of external stimuli may distract them from important tasks at hand. Conversations, noise, television, music, movement, other persons, pets, clutter, the computer, or cell phone may serve as distracting stimuli. Many persons with ADHD struggle to filter out external distractions. They may need relative isolation in order to study, to complete academic assignments, and for doing other tasks that require focused attention. Such children and adolescents may find it difficult to return to the task at hand once distracted. As a result, it may take them longer to study and complete tests and assignments compared with children without ADHD. Taking active efforts to decrease such external distractors is often very important in helping such children at home and school.

Example: Laura is a 17-year-old girl who was identified with an Attention-Deficit/Hyperactivity Disorder during childhood. She says that she has always been easily distracted by things going on around her. This has especially negatively impacted her academic functioning. She states that her Individualized Education Program (IEP) allows her the opportunity to sit in the front of the classroom. This has been helpful given that she would otherwise be distracted by other students, movement, and other things going on around her. Nonetheless, she reports that she is still easily distracted, even with such environmental manipulations. She indicates this is especially the case during exams. She offers examples stating that she is distracted by other students coughing, fidgeting, making noise, and so forth. She finds it difficult to return her focus to test questions if someone asks a question to the teacher during the test. She was recently offered the opportunity to take exams in a reduced distraction environment (i.e., a classroom containing two of her peers who also demonstrate ADHD). Laura says that this was helpful. She comments that she is extremely distracted by her cell phone and by social media. She says that she needs to turn her cell phone off in order to study. Otherwise, she feels compelled to check text messages, Facebook, Twitter, or Snapchat. Laura reports that she needs to isolate herself in her bedroom in order to study and complete homework. She says that she cannot focus otherwise, given that she will be distracted by other family members talking, someone watching TV, her cat, and so forth.

9. *Is often forgetful in daily activities* (e.g., doing chores, running errands; for older adolescents and adults, returning calls, paying bills, keeping appointments).

Children and adolescents demonstrating an Attention-Deficit/ Hyperactivity Disorder are often forgetful in a range of day-to-day activities. They may find it difficult to remember to do what they told themselves to do. Many such children often forget to do what they were told to do by parents, teachers, and others. It is not uncommon for them to forget to bring necessary items to school (e.g., homework, books, binders). Such children may forget to bring home from school similar items. Such children often leave things behind (e.g., coat, glasses, school ID) in a range of locations. They may forget to bring toys and other items into the house at night. Such children may forget directions, instructions, and other things that are communicated. Older adolescents may forget appointments and other obligations. They may forget to return calls; do errands, chores, or paperwork; pick up key items from the store; and so forth.

It is important for the clinician to ensure that any reports of forgetfulness reflect true forgetfulness and not purposeful behavior. Some children and adolescents claim forgetfulness (e.g., in relation to homework, assignments, chores, instructions) when in fact such behavior actually reflects a volitional choice.

Example: Javier is a 15-year-old boy who is referred for neuro-psychological exam by his pediatrician. His parents are concerned regarding inattention and memory difficulties. Javier reports that he often forgets to bring homework and other necessary assignments to school. He says that he always does his homework. He will sometimes leave it on the desk in his room or forget to pack it in his bag. There have also been times where he has brought his homework to school but has forgotten to hand it in. Such behavior has impacted his grades negatively.

Javier often forgets instructions. He also frequently forgets to do what he was asked to do. His mother states that she has tried writing down instructions on paper. This has somewhat helped, yet he often forgets or loses these notes. Javier says that he tries to plan out what he needs to accomplish during the day. He notes that he frequently forgets to do what he tells himself to do. He says that he also often forgets to bring needed equipment to football practice. He reports that he has trouble remembering many plays that were just called in the huddle. Javier says that he can remember basic or short plays. He indicates that he forgets plays that have lengthy sequences. Both he and his parents indicate that he has lost numerous jackets, calculators, sunglasses, toys, and other items over the years as he has frequently forgotten these things in various places. It is also not uncommon for his parents to drive him back to school in the late afternoon to retrieve books, papers, or something else that he needed to bring home but forgot to pack in his bag.

Javier says that he also finds it difficult to remember information that he has read. He denied any reading difficulties and states that he likes to read. He says that he frequently has to reread information a few times over in order to retain what he has read.

Hyperactivity Symptoms/Symptoms of Hyperactivity

1. *Often fidgets with or taps hands or feet or squirms in seat.*

   Many children and adolescents with ADHD fidget excessively. Such fidgeting may take a variety of forms. It is not uncommon for the child to tap their feet, shake their leg, move their legs, fidget with their hands, tap objects with their fingers, or squirm in their seat. Others may fidget with their clothing or hair. Fidgeting may also take the form of having to manipulate or play with some sort of object with their hands. Some children who fidget may rock back and forth in their seat. Other children and adolescents with this symptom sometimes even sway back and forth, or move from leg to leg, when standing and talking to others. Such fidgeting is often very noticeable to others especially when displayed by younger children. Parents may tell their child to stop fidgeting or moving. Similar comments are often made by teachers. Many children and adolescents will indicate that they are more likely to fidget when seated (e.g., in the classroom, while doing homework, in church). Some children who are cognizant that such behavior may be viewed as inappropriate will actively try to resist fidgeting.

   Example: London is an 8-year-old boy who presents with complaints of academic underachievement and disruptive behavior. Teachers have reportedly commented that he constantly fidgets while in the classroom. They have stated that he often taps his feet, shakes his legs, and drums with his hands. During class, he is frequently seen playing with pencils, erasers, paper clips, and other small items at his desk. His father notes similar behaviors at home, during church, and wherever else they may be. London's father states that he fidgets minimally when watching TV or playing video games. He will often fidget while doing homework, eating at the table, and during church services. London's father adds that he frequently tells him to stop fidgeting. He adds that London may stop fidgeting for a short time only. This behavior will usually return after a short period of time. London agrees that he fidgets excessively. He relates that his parents and teachers often tell him to stop fidgeting. He indicates that some of his friends have asked him why he is always fidgeting. London states that he does not know why he fidgets a lot and he cannot help it.

2. *Often leaves seat in situations when remaining seated is expected* (e.g., leaves his or her place in the classroom, in the office or workplace, or in other situations that require remaining in place).

Many children with ADHD find it difficult to sit for extended periods of time. Such children often find it difficult to stay seated in the classroom. They may be out of their seat when it is inappropriate to do so. Others will stand up and then sit back down. Children with this symptom may excessively ask for permission to leave their desk (e.g., to use the restroom, sharpen a pencil). Similar behavior may be displayed at home during the homework process. Such children may also find it difficult to stay seated in other situations such as at the dinner table, in a restaurant, in the movie theater, in the doctor's office, in church, and so forth. Many children and adolescents report that they find it difficult to stay seated in many situations. If possible, some persons will actively avoid situations where extended seating is necessary.

Example: Mai-Lei is a 9-year-old girl who has always had difficulty staying seated in the classroom. Teachers have historically reported that she is frequently out of her seat. She goes to sharpen her pencil multiple times during the day. She may leave her seat to throw something in the trash, come up to the teacher at her desk to ask a question, or may even go talk to another student. Mai-Lei's current teacher says that she usually asks to go to the restroom at least five or six times during the day. Further, Mei-Lei is often gone for an extended amount of time when her teacher has allowed her to the restroom.

Mai-Lei's mother reports that similar behavior is demonstrated when they do homework after school. She is frequently out of her seat at the table where they do homework. She says that Mai-Lei will often stand next to her seat several times during dinner. She adds that they no longer go to movies, theater performances, or other productions because Mai-Lei cannot stay seated for the entire length of the performance. She will often ask to go to the restroom or want to leave. Mei-Lei has also asked her mother to change seats several times during a movie or other performance.

3. *Often runs about or climbs in situations where it is inappropriate.* (In adolescents or adults, this may be limited to feeling restless).

   Many children with ADHD may climb in situations where it is inappropriate to do so. This behavior may be reflected by climbing on the bed or other furniture, various structures, and so forth. Such children often require frequent reminders to walk and not run. They may need reminders from their parents to not run in stores, restaurants, parking lots, and other locations. Such children are often told not to run down the halls in school. Many of these children and adolescents are easily bored. They often need to be busy or to be doing things.

   Running around and climbing excessively in situations where it is inappropriate to do so often decrease during adolescence. Some of these adolescents appear restless. Many will describe feeling physically restless internally or feeling an urge to move.

Example: Travis and Tyler are brothers who are presenting for evaluations of ADHD. Travis is 9 years old, and Tyler is 14 years old. Travis has reportedly received multiple complaints at school for running down the halls. Complaints have been offered because he will run, not walk, when he gets off the school bus. He has continued with such behavior despite both teachers and his parents offering him corrective feedback. His mother says that he is a boy who is constantly running or climbing on things. She indicates that she frequently has to remind him to walk, not run, when he gets out of the car. She often has to tell him to stop running down the aisles at Walmart or when they go grocery shopping. She says that he is constantly jumping on beds and other furniture at home.

Tyler reportedly demonstrated similar behavior when he was Travis's age. However, his mother says that he no longer climbs on things nor runs about excessively. She comments that Tyler frequently seems restless. He does not like sitting still. Tyler says that he purposely does not run around all over the place, or climb on things, because he knows that it is inappropriate. He does not want to get in trouble. He adds that he does not want others to think that he is weird. However, he says that he often feels physically restless, and sometimes feels like doing these things. He agrees that he does not like to stay seated for long periods of time. He reports that he especially feels physically restless and experiences an urge to move in such situations. He will force himself to stay seated because he does not want to get in trouble. Tyler enjoys working out at his school's gym. He reports that regular exercise significantly reduces these feelings of restlessness. He comments that he works out most days of the week because he will likely feel agitated and physically restless if he does not exercise.

4. *Often unable to play or engage in leisure activities quietly.*
Many children and adolescents with ADHD have difficulty doing fun things quietly. They may be excessively loud or boisterous. They may need reminders to lower their volume. Some children with ADHD may be loud when playing alone (e.g., when playing video games), yet this is not always the case. Others may be talking out loud or making noises when engaged in tasks.

Example: Ezekiel is a 12-year-old boy who demonstrates ADHD. He is very social and has a number of friends. No significant behavior problems are reported. However, Ezekiel is often very loud when playing with his friends, when playing video games, and during other fun activities. He is usually excessively loud when playing with others and in some social interactions. Ezekiel states that his friends joke and call him the "loud guy." He acknowledges that he often becomes overly excited and rather loud in many situations. Ezekiel reports that his parents often tell him to lower his voice and volume. Teachers have done the same. He says that even some of his friends have told him that at times he is yelling. Ezekiel indicates that he can get loud when playing video games or board games with others. His mother says that he constantly makes noises when playing alone (e.g., when playing video games). She adds that Ezekiel frequently talks much louder when he is talking to someone, when he gets excited, and when he is having fun. His mother indicates that he has always been this way.

5. *Is often "on the go," acting as if "driven by a motor"* (e.g., is unable to be or is uncomfortable being still for extended time, such as when in a restaurant or a meeting; may be viewed by others as being restless or difficult to keep up with).

Many persons with ADHD find it difficult to relax. They often feel the need to be moving or doing things, or are on the go. Many children with ADHD appear to have bounds of energy. They often seem as if they are driven by a motor. They may become bored easily and need to be engaged in frequent activity. Many struggle to engage in tasks that require them to stay in one location for an extended period of time. Such children may find it difficult to sit through movies, church, class lectures, meals, and other situations where one needs to stay in the same place for an extended period of time.

Example: Bobby is an 8-year-old boy who was recently diagnosed with ADHD by his pediatrician. His current and prior teachers have raised concerns regarding hyperactivity. His parents state that he has bounds of energy, usually needs to be moving, has difficulty relaxing, and appears to be as if he is driven by a motor. Bobby is a boy who reportedly becomes bored easily. He always needs to be engaged in some activity. His parents say that he could easily sit and play video games for more than an hour if allowed to do so. Otherwise, it is quite difficult to keep Bobby engaged in activities for an extended period of time. He will not complete board games as he often seems to lose interest and goes on to something else. His parents report that they no longer go to movies. They note that Bobby easily becomes bored at movies; he will want to change seats, go to the lobby to play video games, or ask to leave. He has similar difficulty sitting through television shows and movies at home. His parents report that they only go to restaurants that are family friendly and where the service is quick. Bobby will become restless after a short period of time, ask to walk around, or indicate that he wants to leave.

6. *Often talks excessively.*

Children and adolescents with ADHD may often talk excessively. Such children may go on and on when conversing with others. They may ramble when they talk or go from topic to topic. Some may start conversations mid-thought and not recognize that the person that they are talking to may not understand the context. Such children often talk significantly more than others. They may talk in class when they should not be talking. They may receive critical feedback from teachers for excessive talking. Some children and adolescents with ADHD may also frequently talk out loud to themselves. Those who do this are often speaking aloud their internal dialogue. Many of these children may receive complaints from others regarding their excessive talking.

Example: Adrianna is a 13-year-old girl who reportedly talks excessively. She states that she often gets in trouble at school due to excessive talking. She says that several of her friends frequently comment that she talks nonstop, and a couple have said that it is sometimes difficult to be around her because of how much she talks. These same friends have also told her that it is often difficult for them to get a word in edgewise. Adriana's mother reports that she has talked excessively since a very young age. Her mother reports that at times it is difficult to follow her thought processes as she may switch from topic to topic. Both Adriana and her mother also report that she often talks aloud to herself and when alone.

Impulsivity Symptoms

1. *Often blurts out an answer before a question has been completed* (e.g., completes people's sentences; cannot wait for turn in conversation). Children and adolescents with ADHD often tend to be verbally impulsive. Such verbal impulsivity may take the form of blurting. Many will blurt out words without first pondering the potential pros and cons. Such children may blurt out answers before the speaker has finished. Some may blurt out answers in class without raising their hand. It is not uncommon for some of these children to seem quite impatient during conversations. They may blurt out words to complete other person's sentences. Many have difficulty waiting their turn in conversations. Many such children and adolescents also frequently make impulsive decisions.

Example: Janera is a 9-year-old girl who reportedly demonstrates some disruptive classroom behaviors. Teachers have repeatedly complained that she rarely raises her hand and will often yell out answers to questions asked in class. Such behavior has also been displayed in her interactions with other children. She often says things without thinking, and this has alienated some of her peers. Her mother says that similar behavior is displayed at home and in other settings. Her mother reports that Janera often becomes impatient in conversations and will try to finish the other person's sentences. Her mother says that she is quite impulsive verbally and frequently says things without thinking.

2. *Often has difficulty waiting his or her turn* (e.g., waiting in line).

   Waiting is very difficult for many children who demonstrate an Attention-Deficit/Hyperactivity Disorder. Such children often become easily frustrated with delays. They may be impatient and want things to occur immediately. Many such children may find it difficult to wait their turn in lines (e.g., in the cafeteria, at the water fountain, in a restaurant, at the movie theater). Some adolescents and children may avoid lines, or choose not to stand in a line, if they perceive they may have to wait too long. Such children may also have difficulty waiting their turn in a conversation, when answering questions in class, and in games and other activities where waiting one's turn is required. Such adolescents often drive too fast and may take impulsive risks.

   Example: Alshon is a 17-year-old boy who is presenting for clinical exam. His parents state that he has always been impulsive. He is impatient and struggles to wait his turn. Alshon indicates that he has been driving for approximately six months. He reports that he has received two speeding tickets to date. He comments that he has been in one minor motor vehicle accident and dented his parents' car when backing out of the driveway when he struck the mailbox. He states that he often becomes impatient when driving. He says that he experiences "road rage" at times, especially if traffic is moving slowly. Alshon states that he may take an alternate route, even if it such a route would take longer, because he cannot stand to wait in traffic. He acknowledges that he also has trouble waiting in lines. He frequently leaves a situation if the line is too long. Alshon says that he will not go to any newly released movies with his friends because he knows that lines will be long and he simply cannot wait in such a line. His parents comment that he has always had difficulty waiting his turn. Alshon remembers that when he was younger he would frequently complain to his parents if he had to wait in a line at an amusement park, at the doctor's office, and in many other situations. Alshon relates that he tries to plan his activities so that he does not have to wait any significant period of time.

3. *Often interrupts or intrudes on others* (e.g., interrupts conversations, games, or activities; may start using other people's things without asking or receiving permission; for adolescents, may intrude into or take over what others are doing).

Impulsivity can also take the form of interrupting or intruding on others. Such children may interrupt their parents talking on the phone. They may force their way into conversations prior to being invited into the conversation. Such children may interrupt during conversations. Interrupting can also take the form of being intrusive. Such children and adolescents may interrupt other persons' games or activities uninvited. They may try to take over the activity. Children displaying such impulsivity may also be intrusive in other ways. Some of these children and youth are often irritable and quick to anger.

Example: Maria is an 8-year-old girl who is presenting for evaluation. Her mother states that she is quite impulsive. She often interrupts others. Examples were given, such as interrupting conversations, interrupting other people's activities, and taking over other children's games without invitation. Maria's mother says that Maria frequently interrupts her when she is talking on the phone or talking to other adults. Teachers and other parents have offered similar feedback. Maria says that some of her friends have complained that she interrupts them when they are talking. Teachers have reported that Maria frequently interrupts others' conversations. She also often interrupts other children's games and activities at recess. She frequently interrupts other children who are trying to complete their classwork. Maria's mother reports that some recent improvements have been achieved as Maria now often says "excuse me" when she wants to ask something. However, where she falls short is that she will say "excuse me" and then spontaneously speak prior to the other person acknowledging this request.

CHAPTER 2

Conceptualization of ADHD

Attention-Deficit/Hyperactivity Disorder (ADHD) is a neurobiological or neurodevelopmental disorder. It is a brain-based condition. It is generally agreed upon that genetic factors serve as a primary etiology contributing to the presentation of ADHD for most persons who demonstrate this condition. A number of environmental variables (e.g., prenatal exposure to tobacco, exposure to toxins) have also been demonstrated to increase the risk of developing ADHD. The interplay of genetic and environmental factors, and how such variables impact one another, can also relate to ADHD and how symptoms are specifically expressed.

A thorough discussion of the etiological variables contributing to the risk of developing ADHD would comprise a book in and of itself. The purpose of the current chapter is to offer a brief and basic understanding of the genetic and environmental etiologies that are related to the diagnosis of ADHD.

Genetic Factors Contributing to ADHD

There is overwhelming evidence indicating that ADHD is a condition that is heavily influenced by genetic variables. Twin, adoption, and family aggregation research studies have demonstrated that 75 percent or more of ADHD variance is accounted for by genetic factors alone (Faraone et al., 2005; Nikolas & Burt, 2010; Thapar et al., 2013). Genetic studies have identified a number of gene variants that likely relate to ADHD. As with many medical, neurological, and psychological disorders, no single gene has been identified that accounts for ADHD. Rather, several different gene variants, likely working in unison, contribute to the variation of ADHD symptomatology that may be expressed (Yang et al., 2013). As such, ADHD is a polygenetic condition. These identified genes include those that affect the regulation of dopamine, norepinephrine, serotonin, and GABA. Other identified genes play an important role in brain development, including during cell proliferation, endpoint transmission, and cell support.

Environmental Factors Contributing to ADHD

A number of environmental variables relate to an increased risk that a child may demonstrate an Attention-Deficit/Hyperactivity Disorder. These environmental factors largely relate to neurotoxin exposure that the developing child may experience in utero. Some other environmental variables of risk relate to postnatal events that have transpired in the child's life.

It is important to consider that no absolute casual relationships can be determined from this body of research given the largely correlational methods of data analyses that are typically employed. Further, the strengths of these correlations sometimes differ between studies, differ based on the variables of interest, and differ depending on the sample and research methods employed. It is also often difficult to control for a range of potential confounding variables in such research, especially when data from large population cohorts are analyzed. One must keep these issues in mind. This body of the literature has demonstrated that specific environmental factors appear to increase the risk for ADHD, but the existence of such variables does not imply that the child will absolutely demonstrate this condition.

Tobacco, Alcohol, and Illicit Drug Use: Among leading environmental factors that are associated with ADHD are maternal smoking and alcohol consumption during pregnancy. Tobacco and alcohol are toxins that can negatively impact the developing fetus. In particular, such neurotoxins can have a negative impact on early brain formation. A relatively large body of research indicates that in utero exposure to tobacco and alcohol is a significant risk factor for ADHD (e.g., see Froehlich et al., 2011; Mick et al., 2002). There is a smaller body of literature suggesting that children who are exposed to certain illicit drugs (i.e., marijuana, cocaine, amphetamines, heroin) in utero are at increased risk for developing ADHD as well (e.g., Eriksson et al., 2000; Morrow et al., 2009; Ornoy et al., 1996; Williams & Ross, 2007).

Antidepressant Use: Antidepressant use during pregnancy has been investigated as a potential risk factor associated with ADHD. Figueroa (2010) analyzed medical claims data from 38,074 U.S. children and families. This study looked at the risk of childhood ADHD in five-year-olds and maternal antidepressant use during pregnancy. A significant correlation was noted between children demonstrating ADHD and in utero exposure to bupropion (i.e., Wellbutrin). Consistent with other studies (e.g., Nulman et al., 1989; Oberlander et al., 2007), there was no significant relation between prenatal exposure to a selective serotonin reuptake inhibitor (i.e., SSRI) and ADHD.

Pregnancy and Birth Variables: Perhaps the largest pregnancy-related factors associated with risk for ADHD are maternal use of tobacco products and alcohol during the pregnancy. Such neurotoxins may potentially negatively affect early brain development in the developing fetus, as previously noted.

Low birth weight (i.e., < 2,500 grams) has repeatedly been demonstrated as a significant risk factor for the development of an Attention-Deficit/ Hyperactivity Disorder (e.g., Mick et al., 2002; Nicholas & Chen, 1981; Schothorst & van Engeland, 1996). It is, however, important to consider that a number of maternal factors can increase the risk of low birth weight. These include the age of the mother at the time of delivery (i.e., younger age), poor maternal nutrition, poor prenatal care, specific maternal medical conditions (e.g., hypertension, cardiac disease), prior low-birth-weight infants, illicit drug use, alcohol use, and tobacco usage.

Barkley (2015) points out that research examining a range of other perinatal difficulties and their relation to ADHD is mixed. Some studies have related in utero hypoxic-ischemic incidents, respiratory distress, and preeclampsia with increased risk for ADHD, while other research has failed to yield similar results. However, other than low birth weight, he notes that there does not appear to be a strong correlation between such factors and ADHD symptoms after other variables (e.g., maternal tobacco/ alcohol use, low socio-economic status) are taken into consideration.

Barkley (2015) indicates that research examining the relationship between maternal stress/anxiety during pregnancy and the subsequent development of ADHD in the child must be cautiously interpreted given a range of potential confounding variables and the correlational nature of this research. He notes a possible link between maternal stress/anxiety during pregnancy and child ADHD, although other key factors (i.e., genetics) may potentially better explain many of these research findings.

Exposure to Pesticides: Polanska, Jurewicz, and Hanke (2013) reviewed the literature to investigate the potential association between ADHD and exposure to various pesticides. Organophosphate pesticides are typically used for agricultural purposes to control for insects. These insecticides are toxicants that target the nervous system of the insect. The authors concluded that their review of the literature indicated that children's exposure to such pesticides was associated with an increased risk to display an Attention-Deficit/Hyperactivity Disorder and a Pervasive Developmental Disorder. They also opined that research appears to indicate a significant risk for ADHD for children who have been exposed to organochlorine pesticides and polychlorinated biphenyls (PCBs). Froehlich et al. (2011) arrived at similar conclusions in an independent examination of the research literature.

Lead Exposure: Postnatal exposure to lead can negatively impact the developing child. Lead can result in adverse effects to a range of body organs and systems, including those involving the central nervous system (i.e., the brain). Lead can potentially affect multiple brain-related neurochemical pathways and functions. This may result in decreased cognitive abilities, including intellectual functioning and attention/concentration. Lead can also interfere with brain development. This is potentially deleterious for children and adolescents who are exposed to this substance given that critical periods of brain development occur during these years.

The Centers for Disease Control (CDC) recommended in 1991 (CDC, 1991) that children with blood lead levels (BLLs) of $\geq$ 10 µg/dL undergo additional testing. No safe BLLs in children have been identified (CDC, 2012). Research examining children with high BLLs (= 70 µg/dL) has shown that such children may demonstrate severe neurologic problems, experience coma, or even die. Neurological problems and behavioral disorders have also been displayed by children with BLLs at or below 5 µg/dL (Raymond & Brown, 2016).

Various studies (e.g., Nigg et al., 2008, 2010; Ha et al., 2009) and reviews (e.g., Froehlich et al., 2011; Polanska, Jurewicz, & Hanke, 2013) consistently show a statistically significant correlation between elevated

BLLs and ADHD-related symptoms. However, results from many studies demonstrate that the strength of these correlations is generally small.

Goodlad, Marcus, and Fulton (2013) performed a meta-analysis examining the relationship between lead exposure in children and adolescents and ADHD. A total of 33 studies published between 1972 and 2010 were analyzed. These combined studies included a total of 10,232 children and adolescents. The average r across studies was .16, and this result was statistically significant (95% CI = .12–.20, Z = 8.09, p < .001) when examining the association between inattentive symptoms and lead exposure. This reflects a small to medium effect size (Cohen, 1988) given that this value equates to d = .32. The average r across studies was .13 and statistically significant (95% CI = .09–.16, Z = 7.22, p < .001) when examining the association between symptoms of hyperactivity/impulsivity and lead exposure. This result reflects a small effect size (Cohen, 1988) given that this value equates to d = .26.

Psychosocial Factors Contributing to ADHD

A number of psychosocial variables have historically been proposed to relate to the development of ADHD (see Barkley, 2015 for a review). These have included parental mental illness, parents demonstrating an overstimulating approach to caring for the child, a range of other family-related environmental factors, poor parenting practices, and other maladaptive parental characteristics. While specific parenting behaviors relate to a risk for both an Oppositional Defiant Disorder and Conduct Disorder, none of these variables have been shown to relate to a risk for developing ADHD. There is also no evidence that watching television, exposure to certain types of television programs, the use of electronic devices, or playing video games significantly relate to an increased risk in a child developing an Attention-Deficit/Hyperactivity Disorder.

The Interaction of Genetic and Environmental Factors in Contributing to ADHD

An Attention-Deficit/Hyperactivity Disorder may emerge solely due to a genetic predisposition or an environmental insult. ADHD can also be a result of the interplay between genetic factors and environmental variables. This is where genes moderate the effects of environmental factors, or conversely, where environmental factors serve to moderate how genes are expressed as behavior. Complex gene–environment interactions (or genotype–environment interactions, G×E) may potentially take place in utero or during one's postnatal development. Such genotype–environmental interactions may result in structural changes in the brain. Their effects on these neural networks can have an impact on subsequent cognitive abilities, emotional functioning, and behavior.

Take, for example, a child who demonstrates a genetic predisposition to demonstrate an Attention-Deficit/Hyperactivity Disorder but whose genome is programmed so that the condition never emerges. The child does not end up developing ADHD. Take the same child whose mother regularly smokes and consumes moderate levels of alcohol during pregnancy. Such environmental factors may trigger this genetic vulnerability and ADHD develops. In such a case ADHD is the product of the interplay between environmental and genetic factors.

Another example illustrating potential gene–environment interactions is lead exposure. Take two children who are exposed to lead during the first several years of life. Both have equal blood lead levels. One child demonstrates a combination of genes that make her vulnerable to the effects of this neurotoxin and goes on to develop ADHD. The other child does not display this genetic vulnerability and subsequently never displays ADHD. This is why it is possible for persons to have very different outcomes despite being subject to similar environmental experiences.

CHAPTER 3

Evaluation and Assessment of Attention-Deficit/ Hyperactivity Disorder

Components of the ADHD Exam

An evaluation of an Attention-Deficit/Hyperactivity Disorder consists of several components. A medical evaluation is needed to ensure that no medical etiologies account for symptom complaints. Examination of ADHD should include a review of pertinent records. Clinical interviews (semistructured or structured) of parents, adolescents, and children are needed. ADHD exams should include behavior observations of the child, administration of psychological/behavioral checklists, and, sometimes, objective psychological or neuropsychological assessment instruments. Feedback sessions with the child and parents, development of a treatment plan, linkage with other providers as necessary, and a written report or summary of the examination are also important parts of the ADHD examination. This chapter outlines and discusses the examination components that are involved when evaluating for ADHD in children and adolescents.

Review of Records

The number of records that are available for review greatly differs among children and adolescents who are presenting for an ADHD evaluation. For some patients, no records may be pertinent or available, while other patients may have an extensive documented history of various neuro-developmental, learning, or psychological concerns.

It is helpful to ask parents to bring pertinent records to the intake session. Such records may include prior psychoeducational evaluations that were completed via the school district, prior neuropsychological/ psychological assessments, any psychological/psychiatric records, pertinent medical records, school records (e.g., report cards, standardized testing, 504 plan, Individualized Education Program), and relevant records from other professionals (e.g., speech/language evaluation, occupational therapy evaluation).

Developmental History

Understanding the child's developmental history is important. This should include questions regarding pregnancy, length of pregnancy, use of substances (e.g., tobacco, drugs, alcohol) during pregnancy, child's birth weight, any birth trauma, and if the child required any specific medical care soon after birth. It is also important to understand a child's developmental course in relation to the usual developmental milestones (e.g., crawling, standing, walking, language, gross/fine motor coordination, social/emotional functioning). If delays were displayed, the evaluations and/or treatments pursued and their outcomes must also be discussed.

Medical History

The ADHD exam includes a thorough understanding of the child's medical history. This should include any current or prior major medical illnesses, injuries, and surgeries. A number of medical conditions can mask as ADHD when ADHD may not actually be present. Other medical etiologies can sometimes play a part in exacerbating ADHD symptomatology. Common conditions to query include head trauma, concussions, hypoxic events, traumatic brain injury, and seizure disorders. The presence of allergies, asthma, diabetes mellitus, cardiac conditions, or a sleep disorder may be important to understand. Children presenting for an ADHD exam should have undergone a relatively recent physical exam to rule out any obvious competing medical etiologies that could account for presenting symptoms. As previously noted, sometimes it may be important to consult with a child's physician in order to understand the potential impact that a specific medical condition may be having on the child's cognition and behavior.

It is important to ensure that children and adolescents undergoing an evaluation for ADHD have relatively recently completed vision and hearing exams. This is important in order to be sure that any "attentional" or learning difficulties are not actually a function of hearing or vision deficits. I always like to ask children and adolescents who require glasses if they actually wear their glasses. It has been my experience that a number refuse to wear their glasses. Others still have either broken or lost their glasses, and their parents have not had them replaced. These issues often need to be addressed as part of the examination process.

Medications

It is helpful to ask parents to bring any prescribed medication to the intake session. Understanding all current and past medication trials, if any, is important in the evaluative process. The evaluating clinician needs to gain an understanding of the efficacy of current and past medication trials. Understanding possible side effects and other potential negative effects is also of interest.

It is often helpful to understand the relative course of any prescribed psychostimulant medication throughout the day. Asking about when this medication seems to begin to metabolize out of the child's system can be helpful. Understanding rebound effects, if any, is of interest. Also, it may be important to understand when the child actually takes his or her medication (e.g., during the school week, on weekends).

An understanding of such medication-related issues can often be helpful in advising treatment planning when children demonstrate functional deficits stemming from ADHD. For example, the child whose extended-release psychostimulant medication has metabolized out of their system by 3:00 p.m. may find it very difficult to focus on after-school tutoring and homework. They may need an additional short-acting psychostimulant agent for after-school and evening study. The child who demonstrates functionally impairing disruptive behavior (e.g., within the family, with his or her social interactions with peers) on weekends only when they do not take their prescribed medication is another common example where medication intervention may be advised.

ADHD is a neurodevelopmental disorder that commonly results in functional academic impairments. The misnomer for many parents is that their child with ADHD requires treatment only during the school week. In reality, ADHD is a condition that can result in other functional impairments such as negatively impacting one's life at home, their friendships, social interactions, job functioning, and participation in recreational activities. It can also impact how they manage daily responsibilities. A functional analysis of such behavior can often be helpful in determining when medication is needed. A number of children and adolescents who display such functional impairments do much better when they take their medication seven days per week.

Substance Use History

The evaluation process should include questions to understand any pertinent substance use issues. This often does not apply to very young children yet certainly applies to most children who are of middle-school age and older. It is often helpful to ask such questions independently to the child and parent. This includes an understanding of any potential use of alcohol, illicit drugs, and tobacco. Understanding the potential use and abuse of over-the-counter medications (e.g., cough medicine, cold medicines, diet pills, sleep medications) is also important.

It is also important to understand if the child has used prescription medications that were not prescribed to him or her. This includes psychostimulant medications (e.g., Adderall, methylphenidate, Ritalin, Concerta, Vyvanse) that have been obtained via diversion. It has been increasingly common for some adolescents and young adults to obtain such medication from a variety of sources. This is not to say that the youth who have engaged in such practices do not demonstrate ADHD. It is within the realm of possibility that ADHD is present. It can sometimes be helpful to ask such adolescents the impact such medication has on them. However, the evaluating clinician must cautiously consider such reports. Relatedly, a positive response to psychostimulant medication does not necessarily imply that the individual demonstrates a DSM-5 diagnosis of an Attention-Deficit/Hyperactivity Disorder. It is not uncommon for many persons to experience some level of cognitive enhancement even though they do not demonstrate ADHD.

Psychological History

Psychological history is important to understand when evaluating for ADHD. It is especially helpful to review prior psychological and/or psychiatric records if available. Asking parents to bring such records to the intake session is ideal. It is important to understand the results of any prior psychological or psychiatric evaluations. Understanding the recommendations that emerged from such exams, recommendations that were actually pursued, and the resultant outcomes is of interest.

Psychological history may also include an understanding of any prior psychological treatments. Understanding why the child pursued treatment, any diagnoses or opinions offered by the treating psychologist or therapist, what interventions were pursued, and what outcomes emerged may be important to understand. This applies equally to any psychiatric treatments that the child has participated in over the years. Also important to understand are the reasons and outcomes of any psychiatric hospitalizations, participation in intensive outpatient psychological treatment programs, substance abuse treatment, or residential placements.

It is important to know if the child has experienced or has been witness to any significant traumatic incidents. Examples include being a victim of physical abuse, sexual abuse, or neglect; experiencing or witnessing a violent crime, serious accident, abduction, hostage situation, terrorist attack, fire, or natural disaster; seeing someone die; and so forth. Such incidents can sometimes elicit specific psychological symptoms (e.g., anxiety, posttraumatic stress) that could mask as attentional symptoms stemming from ADHD. Of course, it is possible for an individual who has experienced any traumatic events to concurrently demonstrate a developmentally based Attention-Deficit/Hyperactivity Disorder.

Educational History

Many children and adolescents with ADHD experience educational difficulties. This is one of the main reasons why such children are referred for an evaluation of ADHD. It is important to understand the child's developmental learning history and functioning. While these academic struggles may relate to untreated ADHD, such academic difficulties could alternatively be a function of one or more competing developmental conditions (e.g., a Specific Learning Disorder), psychological disorder, psychosocial issues, or perhaps motivational variables. Further, ADHD is a condition where comorbidity is the rule rather than the exception. This is why the evaluative process may need to include efforts to clarify one or more potential coexisting conditions that are independent of ADHD.

Obtaining an understanding of the child's educational history can in part be achieved by asking questions pertaining to their current and prior academic functioning. This includes gaining an understanding of any developmental difficulties pertaining to basic letter/word identification skills; phonological processing abilities; language skills such as reading comprehension, spelling, and grammar/sentence structure; math skills; retention of information; and handwriting. Also of interest are prior academic retentions, tutoring, psychoeducational evaluations completed through the school district or elsewhere, other evaluations/services received from the school district (e.g., speech therapy, occupational therapy), 504 Plan, Individualized Education Program, other academic plans, special education services, current grade, and classroom placement.

It is important to understand the actual academic grades that have been obtained by the child. It is always best to review actual report cards and related academic records that provide objective and accurate data. It is also helpful to review any standardized testing that has been completed. It is also of interest to understand the conditions under which the child achieved their grades. For example, a child who is receiving As/Bs with minimal effort, no parental assistance, and no tutoring is likely functioning much differently than a child who is receiving As/Bs but is spending two to three hours every night with a parent reviewing their academic information, receiving other assistance or support with homework and assignments, or attending regular after-school tutoring.

Understanding the child's level of academic effort is often important. While it is common that many children with ADHD often avoid tasks requiring sustained mental effort (e.g., school work and homework)—thus their academic motivation is suboptimal—sometimes poor grades relate solely to poor academic effort and are not a reflection of ADHD or any other identifiable neurodevelopmental condition. Behavioral interventions targeting poor academic motivation may be needed for children and adolescents whether such behavior is rooted in ADHD, other factors, or some combination thereof.

Most schools now offer parents some sort of online portal where they can track their child's progress across subject areas. This typically includes actual grades per task along with overall grades per subject area. Such systems also usually allow for an immediate inspection of what homework/ assignments have been given, along with subsequent grades pertaining to this assigned work. As appropriate, it may be of interest to understand why a parent was not aware of any deficiencies (e.g., the child has not completed multiple homework and other assignments), and/or important to understand the circumstances as to why a parent did not intervene when such dysfunctional behavior has been persistently displayed for an extended period of time. The purpose of the latter is not to egregiously wag the proverbial finger of shame in the direction of the parent. Rather, an understanding of pertinent parent and/or family systems variables is often helpful in guiding treatment recommendations targeting these specific areas of concern.

Academic effort can be understood via an inspection of academic records. It is also helpful to ask parents and children how much time is spent each evening studying or engaging in other assigned academic tasks. Another relatively easy and time-efficient way to assess academic effort is to simply ask the child and parent to rate the child's academic effort during the past six months (e.g., "How would you rate your academic effort over the past six months from 0 to 10? Zero would be the lowest and 10 would be the highest.").

Family History

Research literature indicates a strong genetic predisposition for ADHD. Research has indicated that perhaps 70 to 95 percent of the variance accounted for ADHD relates to genetic variables (Barkley et al., 2002). It is not uncommon for a child who demonstrates ADHD to have a parent or other family member who demonstrates the same condition. It is important to consider that a reasonably larger percentage of adults who have children diagnosed with ADHD may have ADHD themselves that has not been formally diagnosed. It is often important to treat a parent who demonstrates ADHD and, sometimes, to also treat any comorbid psychological conditions displayed, in order for the child with ADHD to make significant progress. It can be helpful to ask parents at some point during the evaluative process if they believe that the discussed ADHD-related symptoms possibly pertain to them or the child's other parent. If so, then sharing this research finding is appropriate. It is often paramount for parents with untreated ADHD to pursue their own evaluation and treatment targeting this condition. It should be emphasized that this is important so that their child can achieve optimal gains. The parent will also probably experience improvements in their general functioning,

It is helpful to separately query potential maternal and paternal familial developmental and psychological histories. Persons of interest should include the child's parents, grandparents, aunts/uncles, immediate cousins, and siblings. It is often important to list potential conditions when making such a query. This may include asking if any persons have actually been diagnosed with such conditions or are suspect in displaying such disorders. Conditions of interest may include ADHD, learning disorders, autism spectrum disorders, other developmental delays, depressive disorders, bipolar disorder, anxiety disorders, Tourette's and other tic disorders, schizophrenia, and substance abuse conditions.

Other Psychosocial History

Other components of the child's psychosocial history are equally important to understand in the process of the ADHD exam. Such issues include where the child has been raised, how often the family has moved, where the child resides currently, family structure, parental functioning, pertinent family systems issues, parent–child interactions, friendships, the child's social relations, potential difficulties with adaptive functioning skills, management strategies employed by parents, if the child has been bullied, and the child's social/interpersonal skills. It may also be important to understand any significant changes or other stressors that have transpired or are ongoing. Other important psychosocial information of interest may include legal history (if any), employment history, and how the adolescent has functioned at work.

Behavior Observations

Behavioral observations of the child are important in any exam of ADHD. A structured protocol can be used. It is usually more practical, and equally acceptable, for the clinician to simply record notes outlining their behavioral observations throughout the examination process. The person making such observations must of course be familiar with behaviors reflecting ADHD symptomatology. This includes an understanding of whether or not the demonstrated behavior is normal or abnormal for the developmental age of the child. Understanding such developmental norms is important. Specific behaviors demonstrated at one age may be normal for the child's developmental level. The same behavior demonstrated at an older age may not.

Examples of common observable behaviors demonstrated by children and adolescents with ADHD are fidgeting, squirming in their seat, leaving their seat, walking around the physician's office and touching various objects, interrupting their parents or the evaluating clinician, looking around the room, other examples of being externally distracted, the clinician needing to repeat questions due to inattention, and verbal hyperactivity. Other observations reflecting internal distractions, jumping from task to task, poor organization, low frustration tolerance, difficulty maintaining attention for longer periods of time, blurting, decreased insight regarding their behavior, reduced social skills, disruptive behavior, and careless errors may also be of interest.

Clinical Interviews for ADHD and Other DSM-5/ICD-10 Conditions

Clinical interviews, whether structured or unstructured, are a primary component of any ADHD exam. Parents, and sometimes children, are interviewed via structured or semistructured methods to understand possible ADHD symptomatology, onset, course, and functional impairments. Structured or unstructured clinical interviews also serve the purpose to understand other possible psychological, neurological, medical, or neurodevelopmental disorders. Sometimes such conditions, and not ADHD, may actually account for the child's symptom complaints. Alternatively, ADHD is a condition where comorbidity is the rule and not the exception. Therefore, it is important to understand all potential psychological contributors to the child's difficulties.

My preference is to employ a structured or semistructured clinical interview when evaluating children and adolescents for a potential

Attention-Deficit/Hyperactivity Disorder. Some clinicians shy away from using such a method as they feel that such instruments are too time consuming. The reality is usually the opposite. An incredibly large amount of information can be obtained from patients in a relatively short amount of time when a structured format is employed. Such a format also better ensures that the clinician can obtain necessary information relevant to the exam. Some patients, especially those with ADHD or those who have parents with ADHD, may ramble, talk off topic, and feel compelled to offer examples and other information. While such information can sometimes be clinically useful, the skilled interviewer needs to obtain as much pertinent information at the intake session as possible and do so quickly and efficiently, while also establishing and maintaining rapport. Such efficiency is especially important given the limitations of managed care. Many patients and their parents also typically respond positively to such a structured format as they feel that the clinician is directly addressing the issues for which they are being examined.

Children and adolescents should usually be included in the interview process in order to gain their perspectives of symptoms, behaviors, and other issues. In general, younger children may be limited informants given their developmental level. Many older children and adolescents often have the capacity to offer reasonably accurate descriptions of symptoms along with the ability to relate other important information. There is, however, significant variance depending on a range of issues. Obtaining information from teachers, tutors, or other persons involved in the child's life is often important. Many such collateral reports are usually obtained via behavior checklists given the limitations of managed care.

A number of excellent semistructured clinical interviews are available when the diagnosis of interest is an Attention-Deficit/Hyperactivity Disorder. Examples include the structured clinical interviews for ADHD offered by Russell Barkley and Kevin Murphy in their publications (Barkley & Murphy, 1998, 2006). These instruments employ the DSM-IV and DSM-IV-TR definitions of ADHD. These structured formats are still relevant for DSM-5 given that only the age of onset has changed in the diagnostic conceptualization of ADHD per DSM-5 definition. The same publications also include structured clinical interviews for a range of other child and adolescent psychological and behavioral disorders using

DSM-IV and DSM-IV-TR diagnostic definitions. The authors generously allow for unlimited use of these clinical interviews for the purchaser of the workbook.

Dr. Susan Young (2015) has developed a semistructured clinical interview for the assessment of ADHD in children and adolescents. This measure also provides a format to collect medical and psychosocial information, along with a structured format to screen a range of other conditions that may accompany ADHD. This instrument is available for free and can be downloaded at www.psychology-services.uk.com.

The M.I.N.I International Neuropsychiatric Interview for Children and Adolescents 7.0 (MINI-KID) and the M.I.N.I International Neuropsychiatric Interview for Children and Adolescents (Parent Version) 7.0 (MINI-KID Parent Version) (Sheehan et al., 2010) provide another structured format for evaluating ADHD. The MINI-KID also allows for the assessment of a range of other DSM-5 psychological and behavioral disorders in a reasonable amount of time. The MINI-KID and the MINI-KID Parent versions are available for purchase at www.medical-outcomes.com.

Other examples of structured instruments that may be used to evaluate ADHD include the Diagnostic Interview Schedule for Children, Version IV (NIMH DISC-IV; Shaffer et al., 2000); Diagnostic Interview for Children and Adolescents, Version IV (DICA-IV; Reich et al., 1996); Child Assessment Schedule (CAS; Hodges et al., 1982); and the Schedule for Affective Disorders and Schizophrenia for School-Age Children, Present and Lifetime Version (K-SADS-PL; Kaufman et al., 1996). These instruments have good psychometric properties. These measures are often employed in research protocols where ADHD is a construct of interest. They may not be practical in most clinical settings given the amount of time required for test administration.

Psychological and Behavioral Instruments for the Evaluation of ADHD

The use of behavioral checklists is standard practice when evaluating a child or adolescent for an Attention-Deficit/Hyperactivity Disorder. Such instruments are typically completed by parents and teachers. It may also be helpful to have an older child or adolescent complete a similar age-appropriate instrument. A number of empirically validated research instruments are available for free or purchase. The decision to use any specific instrument will depend on the purpose of exam, including whether or not other comorbid disorders are a potential concern. This decision-making process may also be influenced by the psychometric properties of the assessment tool to be employed, available normative and/or clinical data, time of administration, scoring ease and time, time involved in data analysis, and cost.

The cost of test administration and scoring has increasingly become a concern for clinicians in the United States especially during the past decade. Practice costs have continued to rise over time, as expected. However, reimbursement rates from the overwhelming majority of insurance carriers have remained stagnant or have declined. Additionally, many insurance carriers have derived other methods to reduce their costs. Such strategies have included authorizing very limited hours for any proposed psychological or neuropsychological testing. Further, some panels are of the opinion that behavior checklists are not reimbursable and should simply be included as part of the initial clinical interview. They feel that the clinician should absorb all associated costs. All of this seems to be the projected trend for the foreseeable future. Clinicians that practice in countries where socialized medicine is the norm (e.g., Canada, United Kingdom) face similar, and perhaps greater, financial struggles.

The purpose of this section is not to lament practice costs. It is true that test publishers sometimes, yet not always, spend considerable funds developing test instruments and scoring programs. They should be fairly compensated for their product. However, it is also my opinion that test publishers need to be cognizant of the increasing financial barriers that psychologists, psychiatrists, therapists, physicians, and other providers face in their attempt to provide optimal patient care while concurrently balancing this financial tightrope. Those that fail to recognize this harsh reality risk going by the wayside. The clinicians who provide ADHD-related assessment and/or treatment services for children and adolescents increasingly have to weigh out the cost–benefit ratio of any instruments employed in their practice.

The following is a brief overview of several instruments that are help-ful in assessing symptoms related to ADHD as part of an assessment battery or for monitoring treatment efficacy. Some of these instruments concurrently allow for an evaluation of a range of comorbid conditions that may be of interest. By no means is this overview exhaustive, and there are other empirically sound assessment instruments available that are not presented here.

Brown Attention-Deficit Disorder Scales (BADDS)

The Brown Attention-Deficit Disorder Scales (Brown, 1996; Brown, 2001) are self-report behavioral checklists that are helpful in identify-ing the presence of an Attention-Deficit/Hyperactivity Disorder. As with a number of other scales developed prior to DSM-5, this instrument continues to be relevant given that DSM-5 symptoms comprising the diagnosis of ADHD remain unchanged.

The Brown Attention-Deficit Disorder Scales for Children and Ado-lescents (Brown, 2001) comprise two age cohorts: children ages 3 to 7 years and children ages 8 to 12 years. Rating forms can be completed by both parents and teachers. A self-report form for children ages 8 to 12 years is also available. The childhood measure includes 50 items. The Brown Attention-Deficit Disorder Scales (Brown, 1996) is a similar instrument targeting adolescents (12 to 18 years) and adults. This instrument con-tains 40 items. The adolescent and adult self-report forms can also be distributed to collateral informants (e.g., parents, teachers). The Brown Attention-Deficit Disorder Scales for Children and Adolescents (Brown, 2001) and Brown Attention-Deficit Disorder Scales (Brown, 1996) are two independent instruments with separate manuals. The psychometric properties of both instruments are solid. The manual is needed in order to calculate age-based scores. However, a scoring program is available for purchase from Pearson Assessments (www.pearsonassessments.com; 800-328-5999). Pearson has not yet offered Q Local or Q-global scoring options for the BADDS at the time of this book's publication.

Attention-Deficit/Hyperactivity Disorder is a complex neurodevelop-mental condition that is characterized by executive dysfunction. ADHD is a condition that may negative impact a range of executive abilities that are important in planning, organization, prioritizing, controlling one's emotions, initiating behavior, changing behavior, and problem solving (Barkley, 2000; Brown, 2006). An understanding of the child's ADHD may possibly involve an examination of executive functions over and above symptoms relating to inattention, hyperactivity, and impulsivity.

The BADDS is an instrument that helps to understand the executive functioning of the child or adolescent who is being rated. An understanding of potential executive dysfunction may be helpful for both assessment and treatment purposes. The Brown Attention-Deficit Disorder Scales for Children and Adolescents yield the following six executive function clusters. The Brown Attention-Deficit Disorder Scales include only Clusters 1 through 5.

Clusters of Executive Functions Assessed by the BADDS

1. *Activation*—Organizing, Prioritizing, and Activating to Work
2. *Attention*—Focusing, Sustaining, and Shifting Attention to Tasks
3. *Effort*—Regulating Alertness, Sustaining Effort, and Processing Speed
4. *Emotion*—Managing Frustration and Modulating Emotions
5. *Memory*—Utilizing Working Memory and Accessing Recall
6. *Action*—Monitoring and Self-Regulating Action

The BADDS also contains traditional summary scales that can be helpful in identifying the diagnosis of ADHD. These same scales can be used in evaluating treatment efficacy. Age-based norms are used to calculate T-Scores from raw scores. The Brown Attention-Deficit Disorder Scales for Children and Adolescents yield two additional scales called *ADD Inattention Total* and *ADD Combined Total Score*. The ADD Inattention Total reflects a summation of the raw scores from Clusters 1 to 5. The ADD Combined Total Score is calculated by summing the raw scores of Clusters 1 to 6. The Brown Attention-Deficit Disorder Scales only have an ADD Total Score given that this measure does not include Cluster 6 of the presented Executive Functions model.

The Brown Attention-Deficit Disorder Scales for Children and Adolescents and the Brown Attention-Deficit Disorder Scales are available from Pearson Assessments (www.pearsonassessments.com; 800-328-5999).

Adolescent Psychopathology Scale (APS)

The Adolescent Psychopathology Scale (Reynolds, 1998) is a child/adolescent self-report measure that is helpful in understanding adolescent psychopathology, personality, and a range of social/emotional problems and competencies. This includes ADHD, along with a gamut of psychological and behavioral disorders that may accompany this condition for many youth. This instrument can be used with adolescents who are ages 12 through 19 years old. One must take into consideration that this instrument employs the DSM-IV diagnostic criteria for such conditions. Nonetheless, it remains a potentially useful measure given that the DSM-5 diagnosis for ADHD is unchanged except for the age of onset, and most childhood and adolescent DSM-5 diagnoses are either unchanged or closely mirror their DSM-IV counterparts.

The APS is comprised of 40 distinct scales. These scales examine various domains of psychological functioning. These include a wide range of Clinical Disorders (20 scales), Personality Disorders (5 scales), and Psychosocial Problem Content areas (11 scales). This instrument also contains validity scales to assist in objectively examining a respondent's response style.

The APS has excellent psychometric properties, including a high level of content validity with respect to DSM-5 diagnostic criteria, good test-retest reliability, excellent internal consistency of its scales, good construct validity, good discriminant validity, and good criterion-related validity. Administration time is approximately 45 to 60 minutes.

The APS is available from Psychological Assessment Resources (PAR); www4.parinc.com, 800-331-8378. A scoring program is available for purchase. The APS can also be administered and scored via PAR's online PAR.iConnect platform.

Behavior Assessment Scale for Children (BASC)

The Behavior Assessment System for Children—Second Edition (Reynolds & Kamphaus, 2004) is a well-established measure that was updated from its original format (BASC; Reynolds & Kamphaus, 1992). Cecil Reynolds and Randy Kamphaus have recently published their third iteration of the BASC (BASC-3; Reynolds & Kamphaus, 2015). Both instruments demonstrate excellent psychometric properties. The BASC-2 and BASC-3 can be employed with children and adults from ages 2 through 25 years.

The BASC-3 has both Teacher and Parent Rating Scales. Both instruments allow for an understanding of potential adaptive and problem behaviors. There is also a Self-Report of Personality measure that can be administered to the patient. This measure is appropriate for persons 8 through 25 years. This measure provides insight regarding the examinee's thoughts and feelings.

The BASC-3 also has an optional module that provides a structured format for qualified clinicians to code and record direct observations of a child's behavior in a classroom setting. In particular, this can be useful in determining the presence or absence of behaviors associated with ADHD. Further, the BASC-3 has an option to employ a structured interview in order to obtain specific medical, educational, developmental, psychological, and social history pertaining to the child being examined.

The BASC-3 is especially helpful in the evaluation of an Attention-Deficit/Hyperactivity Disorder. Equally, this measure can be helpful in objectively examining the efficacy of treatments targeting ADHD. Separate scales examine symptoms of ADHD-related hyperactivity and inattention. The BASC-3 also examines a range of clinical, psychosocial, and adaptive behavioral concerns that often coexist for many children and adolescents with ADHD. These include anxiety, depression, somatization, aggression, conduct problems, atypical psychological symptoms, social skills, functional adaptive behavior, and functional communication.

The BASC-3 allows for a better understanding of executive functioning. As previously discussed, ADHD is a neurodevelopmental condition that is characterized by executive deficits. An understanding of such deficits may be important in both the assessment and treatment of this condition. The BASC-3 includes an examination of four distinct areas of executive functioning. These include: (1) Problem Solving Index; (2) Attentional Control Index; (3) Behavioral Control Index; and (4) Emotional Control Index. An Overall Executive Functioning Index is calculated by summing the raw scores of these four indexes.

A scoring program is available for the BASC-2. Pearson offers a variety of methods for administering and scoring the BASC-3. Manual test administration and scoring options are available. A few different unlimited-use scoring subscriptions are available for purchase. Options for online administration and scoring of the BASC-3 via Pearson's Q-global platform are also available.

The BASC-2 and BASC-3 can be purchased from Pearson Assessments (www.pearsonassessments.com; 800-328-5999).

Disruptive Behavior Rating Scale (DBRS)—Parent Form and Teacher Form

The Disruptive Behavior Rating Scale—Parent Form and Disruptive Behavior Rating Scale—Teacher Form (Barkley & Murphy, 2006) are brief assessment tools that are helpful in identifying an Attention-Deficit/Hyperactivity Disorder, Oppositional Defiant Disorder, and Conduct Disorder. These measures are comprised of the 18 symptoms constituting the diagnosis of ADHD and the 8 symptoms that relate to diagnosis of Oppositional Defiant Disorder. The Parent Form only also contains the 15 symptoms that comprise the diagnosis of Conduct Disorder. These measures continue to be relevant for DSM-5 given that the symptoms of ADHD, Oppositional Defiant Disorder, and Conduct Disorder are unchanged from DSM-IV-TR.

Parents and teachers are asked to provide ratings that best describe the behavior of the child during the past six months. Ratings include 0 (Never or rarely), 1 (Sometimes), 2 (Often), and 3 (Very Often). Parents are asked to rate "Yes" or "No" if in the past 12 months their child has engaged in any of the 15 behaviors comprising the diagnosis of Conduct Disorder.

The ADHD norms for this scale are presented by the authors in the workbook. They note that the norms for this scale are the same as those for the ADHD Rating Scale-IV (DuPaul, Power, Anastopoulos, & Reid, 1998), which is an excellent empirically sound instrument in its own right. The ADHD Rating Scale-IV is essentially identical to the ADHD evaluative format of the DBRS. The *ADHD Rating Scale-IV* is available via the Guilford Press (www.guilford.com). This publication contains the ADHD Rating Scale-IV, normative data, and psychometric properties of this instrument.

The DBRS is published in Barkley and Murphy's 2006 publication *Attention-Deficit Hyperactivity Disorder—A Clinical Workbook, Third Edition*. This workbook also includes some other checklists that may be helpful in evaluating ADHD and associated conditions that often accompany this diagnosis. These checklists include a screening checklist for ADHD, measures assessing specific behavioral difficulties at home and school, history forms for parents to complete, and handouts outlining a range of behavior modification strategies. This workbook further contains similar ADHD instruments and other checklists for evaluating adults presenting for an examination of an Attention-Deficit/Hyperactivity Disorder. The authors generously allow the purchaser of the workbook to photocopy the DBRS and all other checklists and handouts as long as it is for their own personal use with their own clients and patients. This publication is available via the Guilford Press (www.guilford.com).

Barkley Deficits in Executive Functioning Scale—Children and Adolescents (BDEFS-CA)

The Barkley Deficits in Executive Functioning Scale—Children and Adolescents (Barkley, 2012) is a newer instrument that is designed to evaluate the major components of executive functioning in daily life activities of children ages 6 to 17 years. ADHD is a disorder of executive functioning. Difficulties stemming from ADHD often far exceed symptoms of inattention, impulsivity, and hyperactivity. Understanding the child's executive functions can be helpful in identifying a potential Attention-Deficit/Hyperactivity Disorder and in guiding treatment initiatives.

The BDEFS-CA is a valuable tool in both the assessment and treatment planning phases for children who may demonstrate an Attention-Deficit/Hyperactivity Disorder. This instrument may also be helpful when evaluating the executive abilities of children with a range of competing conditions (e.g., Autism Spectrum Disorder, Traumatic Brain Injury, Seizure Disorder).

This instrument contains both short- and long-form administration options. Symptom ratings are offered by parents. The short form contains 20 questions that pertain to the child's executive functioning. The short form yields an overall *Executive Functioning Summary Score* and *Executive*

Functioning Symptom Count. The BDEFS-CA long form is comprised of 70 questions. The long form of this instrument contains the same summary scores as the short form. The long form also contains measures examining five distinct areas of executive functioning. The five factors examining aspects of executive functioning are as follows:

1. *Self-Regulation of Emotion.* Many children with ADHD have difficulties regulating their emotions. Such children can be emotionally reactive and have considerable difficulty in calming themselves down when they are emotional. This factor is helpful in identifying children who display such challenges. Symptoms comprising this factor include difficulties with emotional control. These include problems with not being able to be reasonable when emotional, difficulties distracting oneself from what is upsetting him or her, difficulty calming down when one is emotionally upset, and problems redirecting one's emotions.

2. *Self-Organization/Problem Solving.* This factor contains items reflecting a child's difficulty with processing information quickly or accurately, trouble explaining his or her ideas, difficulties explaining things in their proper order or sequence, and struggles with coming up with solutions to problems.

3. *Self-Management to Time.* This factor pertains to difficulties with sense of time and one's self-management to time. Items comprising the scale pertain to procrastination, poor sense of time, poor time management, difficulties with planning ahead, initiating behavior, and problems with judging how much time various tasks may take or how long it may take to get someplace.

4. *Self-Motivation.* This factor examines the construct of motivation. Items comprising this factor include difficulties with willpower, self-determination, persistence, inconsistent quality or quantity of work performance, appearing unmotivated, and not putting much effort into daily responsibilities (e.g., school work, homework, chores).

5. *Self-Restraint.* Many children with ADHD have difficulty inhibiting various behaviors. Such children are often impulsive with their thoughts and behavior. This scale is helpful in identifying children

who demonstrate such difficulties. Items comprising the scale reflect various aspects of self-restraint difficulties such as acting without considering potential consequences, verbal impulsivity, impulsive decision making, difficulties with inhibiting reactions to events or others, and troubles following the rules in a situation.

The BDEFS-CA long form also allows for calculating the ADHD-EF Index. This Index is comprised of 10 symptoms of the BDEFS-CA that achieved a 97 percent overall accuracy classification (i.e., 70 percent of ADHD cases and 99 percent of controls). Barkley cautions that this index score alone should not be used to diagnose ADHD, and that it is not a substitute for a clinical evaluation of this condition. He notes that statistically elevated ADHD-EF Index scores should be interpreted as an indicator that the child or adolescent is at risk for ADHD.

The BDEFS-CA manual also contains a structured clinical interview of 20 symptoms reflecting various aspects of executive functioning. The author notes that this interview may be helpful when the person being evaluated is unable to complete questionnaires due to an inability to read (or read English) or perhaps demonstrates significant visual impairment.

The psychometric properties of the BDEFS-CA are excellent. The manual is well written and well organized. The BDEFS-CA is very reasonably priced. The actual cost of this instrument is significantly lower than that of other comparable assessment tools. Additionally, Dr. Barkley generously allows the purchaser of the BDEFS-CA to photocopy as many BDEFS-CA instruments from the manual as desired as long as it is for personal use or use with individual clients. The BDEFS-CA is available for purchase from the Guilford Press (www.guilford.com).

Achenbach System of Empirically Based Assessment (ASEBA)— Child Behavior Checklist

The Achenbach System of Empirically Based Assessment instruments (Achenbach & Rescorla, 2000, 2001) are widely used in the assessment of ADHD and other psychological conditions when evaluating children and adolescents. Rating forms for parents and teachers are available if the child of interest is of preschool age (i.e., ages 1.5 to 5 years). School-age children can be evaluated via parent rating instruments (Child Behavior Checklist/6 to 18 years) and teacher rating instruments (Teacher Report Form). A separate self-report instrument (i.e., Youth Self-Report/11 to 18 years) is available for older children and adolescents in order to gain their self-report of symptoms and behavior.

These measures yield self-reported competency of the child (e.g., as it relates to academic achievement, social functioning, participation in activities). Each measure contains eight empirically-based syndrome scales. These scales are titled Anxious/Depressed, Withdrawn/Depressed, Somatic Complaints, Social Problems, Thought Problems, Attention Problems, Rule-Breaking Behavior, and Aggressive Behavior. Each measure also yields six DSM-oriented scales that are consistent with DSM-5 categories. These scales are titled Depressive Problems, Anxiety Problems, Somatic Problems, Attention-Deficit/Hyperactivity Problems, Oppositional-Defiant Problems, and Conduct Problems. Two other scales entitled Obsessive-Compulsive Problems and Posttraumatic Stress Problems round out this instrument. These scales can be helpful in identifying symptoms associated with these psychological conditions that co-occur for a percentage of children who display ADHD. The Preschool CBCL also contains an Autism Spectrum Problems Scale that is comprised of items that are consistent with DSM-5 criteria for an Autism Spectrum Disorder.

In relation to ADHD, the Attention Problems Scale and Attention-Deficit/Hyperactivity Problems Scale can be useful in identifying symptoms that may represent this condition. Items loading on these scales are consistent with symptoms that comprise the ADHD DSM-5 defined diagnosis. There is an additional scale, titled Sluggish Cognitive Tempo. This scale may possibly be helpful in identifying symptoms that relate to this proposed variant of ADHD.

There is plentiful research literature illustrating the excellent reliability and validity properties of this instrument along with its clinical utility (e.g., Achenbach & Rescorla, 2000; Achenbach & Rescorla, 2001; Achenbach & Ruffle, 2000; Achenbach, 2009; Achenbach, Rescorla, & Ivanova, 2012). Scoring options include multicultural normative group comparisons. Computer and web-based scoring options are available. These scoring programs also offer narrative reports that describe the child's profile. It is also possible to perform cross-informant comparisons (i.e., ratings offered by parents, teachers, and the child).

The ASEBA measures are available via several major test publishers and other distributors. They can be purchased directly from ASEBA via their website (www.aseba.org).

Clinical Assessment of Behavior (CAB)

The Clinical Assessment of Behavior (Bracken & Keith, 2004) is an instrument that can be helpful in identifying children and adolescents who demonstrate a range of developmental, behavioral, psychiatric, and learning difficulties. This includes a potential Attention-Deficit/Hyperactivity Disorder. It is perhaps important to consider that this instrument's development employed a DSM-IV-TR conceptualization. Nonetheless, it continues to demonstrate useful clinical utility given that a large number of childhood DSM-5 diagnoses, including ADHD, largely mirror or are identical to their DSM-IV-TR counterparts.

This instrument is appropriate for children ages 2 through 18 years. Parents provide ratings via either the Parent Extended Form (CAB-PX) or the shorter Parent Form (CAB-P). Teacher ratings can be obtained via the Teacher Form (CAB-T), which contains matched items. The CAB manual presents data reflecting good reliability and validity statistics in relation to this instrument.

Parent ratings and teacher ratings yield a variety of scores. The Clinical Scales are comprised of three summary behavioral realms of interest. These scales are titled Internalizing Behaviors, Externalizing Behaviors, and Critical Behaviors. Ratings also provide insights regarding adaptive behavioral functioning. The Adaptive Scales are comprised of three such areas of interest including scales titled Social Skills, Competence, and Adaptive Behaviors. The CAB provides information regarding 10 distinct clinical areas of interest that pertain to specific psychological disorders and other clinically significant behaviors. These scales comprise the Clinical Clusters. The specific scales are titled Anxiety, Depression, Anger, Aggression, Bullying, Conduct Problems, Attention-Deficit/Hyperactivity, Autistic Spectrum Behaviors, Learning Disability, and Mental Retardation.

The CAB includes two other Cluster Scales of potential interest. These fall under the categorization of Adaptive Clusters. The Executive Function cluster helps to understand aspects of the child's executive functioning. Items pertaining to planning, judgment, self-regulation, following multistep instructions, and persistence comprise this scale. Such information may be helpful in identifying ADHD when one considers that ADHD is a spectrum disorder involving aspects of executive dysfunction. Further, understanding the child's specific executive difficulties may be helpful in educational and other treatment planning. The second cluster scale that falls under the Adaptive Clusters realm is entitled Gifted and Talented. Items comprising this scale include a number of characteristics that are displayed by gifted and talented children. These include items reflecting specific learning abilities, interpersonal skills, self-confidence, and decision making.

The CAB is published by PAR (www.4parinc.com; 800-331-8378). The CAB can be scored via a traditional computer-based scoring program or by PAR's online PARiConnect platform.

Conners Third Edition (Conners 3)

The Conners 3 (Conners, 2008) is an instrument that is helpful in identifying symptoms and behaviors associated with an Attention-Deficit/Hyperactivity Disorder. This measure also helps to understand a range of symptoms, behaviors, and other concerns that often accompany this condition. The psychometric properties of the Conners 3 are excellent. Short and long forms are available. Parent forms and teacher forms allow for ratings of children and adolescents ages 6 to 18 years. A self-report version of the Conners 3 is available for children and adolescents ages 8 to 18 years. Hand-scoring and computer-scoring options are available.

The Conners 3 is one of the few measures that incorporate validity scales. The full version includes validity scales examining inconsistent responding, positive impression, and negative impression. This allows for an objective assessment of an overly positive or overly negative response bias, along with an objective manner in which to determine if the examinee responded to test items in a consistent manner.

The Conners 3 has summary indexes that are helpful in identifying the presence of ADHD, specific variant of ADHD, level of symptom severity, and severity of associated functional impairments.

Separate scales assessing symptoms of inattention and hyperactivity/ impulsivity comprise the instrument. The Conners 3 also contains scales that are helpful in understanding a range of externalizing behavioral disorders that frequently accompany ADHD (i.e., Oppositional Defiant Disorder, Conduct Disorder). Relatedly, items assess for behaviors reflecting verbally and physically aggressive behaviors. This instrument contains screening questions that are helpful in understanding possible depressive and anxiety-related issues.

A subgroup of children with ADHD struggle with their interpersonal interactions and relationships. The Conners 3 Peer Relations Scale helps to understand if the child demonstrates such challenges. This scale examines problems with friendships, problems with social skills, limited social connections, and difficulty being accepted by one's peer group.

A relatively large number of children with ADHD have comorbid learning disorders or other learning difficulties. The Learning Problems Scale helps to identify children who display difficulties with reading, spelling, or math, or who struggle to remember concepts and may need extra instruction. This scale may be helpful in identifying children who may require psychoeducational or neuropsychological assessment in order to rule out a Specific Learning Disorder.

ADHD is a neurodevelopmental condition that involves executive dysfunction. The Conners 3 allows for a more in-depth understanding of the child's executive functions via items directed at such processes. The Executive Functioning Scale helps to identify specific executive deficits that may be present, including difficulty starting and finishing projects and completing projects at the last minute. Items also help to identify those children who display poor planning, prioritization, and organization.

The Connors 3 is available through Multi-Health Systems (MHS) via their website (www.mhs.com) or the following phone numbers: 1-800-456-3003 (United States); 1-800-268-6011 (Canada); 1-416-492-2627 (from outside North America).

Vanderbilt ADHD Diagnostic Rating Scale

The Vanderbilt Attention-Deficit/Hyperactivity Disorder Diagnostic Rating Scale is a widely used instrument that is helpful in identifying ADHD in children and adolescents. This instrument is also helpful in understanding symptoms and behaviors pertaining to an Oppositional Defiant Disorder, Conduct Disorder, depression, anxiety, academic performance, and other classroom behaviors. Rating scales for parents and teachers are available. Research has indicated that this instrument has relatively good psychometric properties (e.g., Bard et al., 2013; Wolraich et al., 1998, 2003).

The Vanderbilt ADHD Parent Diagnostic Rating Scale includes all 18 DSM-5 behaviors for ADHD. This instrument also contains eight DSM-5 behaviors that comprise the Oppositional Defiant Disorder Scale. A 12-item Conduct Disorder Scale and 7-item anxiety and depression screen make up the remaining test questions. Parents are asked to rate their child's behavior on a 4-point scale with ratings 0 (Never), 1 (Occasionally), 2 (Often), and 3 (Very Often). Additional items rating academic performance, relationships with others, and participation in organized activities are included.

The Vanderbilt ADHD Teacher Diagnostic Rating Scale also includes all 18 DSM-5 behaviors for ADHD. This version contains fewer questions evaluating behaviors related to Oppositional Defiant Disorder and Conduct Disorder. A total of 10 questions comprise a combined scale (i.e., Oppositional Defiant Disorder/Conduct Disorder Screen) examining such disruptive behavior. An additional seven items are included as a screen for anxiety and depression. Teachers are also asked to offer ratings in regard to the child's academic performance and specific classroom behavioral performance.

SNAP-IV Rating Scale

The SNAP-IV Rating Scale is a revision of the Swanson, Nolan, and Pelham (SNAP) Questionnaire (Swanson et al., 1983). This instrument is based on the DSM-IV criteria for ADHD. This instrument remains relevant given that individual symptoms comprising this condition are unchanged in DSM-5. This instrument is also helpful in screening a range of other DSM-5 behavioral and psychological disorders. The evaluating clinician is cautioned that these items are also based on DSM-IV criteria. However, many childhood psychological disorders remain unchanged in the DSM-5 revision, as previously discussed. This questionnaire can be completed by parents or teachers. The same instrument is given to either.

Neuropsychological Assessment

Neuropsychological assessment instruments help to gain an objective understanding of an individual's neurocognitive abilities. Neuropsychological testing is not necessary to establish a diagnosis of ADHD. The administration of such instruments is usually not needed when a diagnosis of ADHD is clear per review of records, developmental history, clinical interviews, clinical observations, and behavior checklists. In many cases, neuropsychological test data does not add any additional useful information in establishing the diagnosis of ADHD when the disorder is evident per the aforementioned assessment methods.

There are situations where such objective assessment of brain functioning may be helpful in determining whether a diagnosis of ADHD is truly present. Neuropsychological testing may be helpful in the assessment process when records, history, observations, interviews, and behavior checklists do not clearly indicate whether the child in question demonstrates ADHD. This may occur in cases where borderline significant symptom reports are offered. For example, borderline or subclinical symptom reports of inattention are sometimes offered by adults (i.e., parents, teachers) when rating children of above-average intelligence who are academically underachieving but not actually receiving poor or failing grades. Neuropsychological assessment may be helpful in identifying or refuting an ADHD diagnosis when there is significant disagreement between informants (e.g., mother vs. father; parents vs. teachers) in relation to reported ADHD symptoms. Relatedly, ADHD is sometimes difficult to ascertain in some children who solely display symptoms associated with the inattentive variant of this condition, and where no disruptive behavioral complaints are offered. Neuropsychological assessment may also be helpful in the differential diagnosis when there are suspicions of competing neurodevelopmental or psychological conditions (e.g., Autism Spectrum Disorder, Mood Disorder, Anxiety Disorder, or some combination thereof) that could better account for the child's symptom complaints in lieu of true ADHD. It is also possible that a child can simultaneously demonstrate ADHD with one or more of such conditions. This is actually not uncommon given that ADHD is a condition where comorbidity is often the norm rather than exception. In sum, neuropsychological evaluation may be helpful in sorting out such complex diagnostic challenges in select cases.

Neuropsychological testing may be necessary when there is concern of ADHD with a potential comorbid Specific Learning Disorder. A recent review of 17 studies (2001 to 2011) by DuPaul, Gormley, and Laracy (2013) examining the co-occurrence of ADHD and Specific Learning Disorders revealed a comorbidity rate of 45.1 percent. This data has significant implications for clinical practice. Children and adolescents presenting with concerns of one of these disorders should be screened for symptoms of the other condition. Further, the academic achievement of children identified and treated for ADHD should be monitored. An examination to rule out a comorbid learning disability should be considered if significant academic improvements are not achieved despite what appears to be reasonable ADHD-related symptom control.

Data emerging from neuropsychological assessments for ADHD may sometimes be helpful in allowing the child or adolescent to access special education services at school (e.g., Individualized Education Program, 504 Plan) and/or testing accommodations (e.g., SAT, ACT). In cases where testing accommodations are being pursued, it is important for the examiner to be familiar with the specific issues that need to be addressed in such an exam, the psychological or neuropsychological tests that must be administered, and the format of the issued report. The same issues apply when adults are seeking testing accommodations (e.g., GRE, MCAT, LSAT, Bar Exam). Such guidelines are typically listed on the websites of the organizations that administer these standardized tests.

Another issue to consider when employing neuropsychological tests is the length of the battery. The examining psychologist or neuropsychologist should keep the testing battery as brief as possible yet still be able to answer the specific question or questions of interest. Data from extensive neuropsychological batteries can provide interesting academic information regarding a child's neurocognitive abilities. Such extensive test batteries are often not necessary, especially when the construct of interest is solely ADHD or perhaps ADHD with a potential comorbid psychological disorder (e.g., Anxiety Disorder, Mood Disorder) or Specific Learning Disorder (e.g., dyslexia, dysgraphia, dyscalculia). Such data is often not understood by nonpsychologists. Such data may not be useful in actual medical, psychiatric, psychological, or educational treatment planning. Further, the financial costs of many lengthy test batteries cannot be justified. However, more extensive test batteries may sometimes be justifiable in complex diagnostic cases, in cases where prior treatments and interventions have failed, or in cases where such data may serve to guide detailed treatment or educational plans. Larger neuropsychological test batteries may also be needed in some cases to assist the child in accessing services. In particular, such lengthy test batteries are often needed in order to access testing accommodations at certain academic levels (e.g., SAT, ACT, college).

The following domains are typically of interest when employing neuropsychological and/or psychological tests in the process of evaluating ADHD and comorbid conditions of interest. Examples of some specific tests within each domain are also offered.

Testing Effort: Adequate testing effort must be offered by the examinee in order to understand the obtained neuropsychological test data. Suboptimal testing effort or purposeful cognitive malingering may invalidate such data.

Issues pertaining to testing effort and cognitive malingering are primarily discussed in the adult literature. It usually is not necessary to administer symptom validity tests to children. Rarely is there a circumstance where secondary gain is an issue. It is also usually quite obvious to the psychologist performing the exam when children are not offering full effort.

Malingering of ADHD is a potential issue when examining older adolescents and young adults. Relatively high rates of malingering have been reported in studies of college students presenting for ADHD and/or ADHD and Learning Disorder exams. Sullivan, May, and Galbally (2007) identified 24.5 percent of their sample to display such behavior during evaluation. A total of 31 percent of students presenting for ADHD evaluations were determined to have volitionally offered noncredible testing effort on neuropsychological tests per two other independent studies (Alfano & Boone, 2007; Suhr et al., 2008). Such poor testing effort raises significant concerns regarding malingering.

Malingering of ADHD symptoms and related purposeful poor testing effort is often motivated by secondary gain factors. These often include obtaining a prescription for stimulant medication, accessing academic and testing accommodations (e.g., in high school, college), or being granted testing accommodations for specific standardized tests (e.g., AP exams, SAT, ACT, GRE, LSAT, MCAT). Information regarding ADHD and its DSM-5 diagnostic criteria are readily available on the Internet. Therefore, it is sometimes difficult to determine the validity of complaints offered by some older adolescents and young adult patients based on clinical interviews and behavior checklists alone. This may be even more problematic when the evaluating professional is faced with time constraints.

Potential malingering should be considered in this population when the patient struggles to offer examples of their claimed symptoms and developmental course of such symptoms. Symptom reports may also be suspect when the individual cannot describe functional impairments stemming from such claimed symptoms, or the only reported functional impairments relate to aspects of their academic functioning (e.g., they are unable to focus in class or when studying; they have trouble completing exams within standard time limitations; they procrastinate or have trouble finding motivation to study). Malingering may also be a concern when there are significant disagreements between symptoms and functional deficits as reported by the patient versus collateral informants (e.g., parents, teachers), and/or when there is limited objective data to support the symptom claims offered by the youth. In such cases, objective neuropsychological assessment may possibly be helpful in determining the presence or absence of ADHD.

Symptom validity tests should be a component of the neuropsychological testing battery for most older adolescents at minimum. Actuarial instruments examining testing motivation should be included in any test battery where the purpose of exam is to potentially obtain academic and/ or testing accommodations.

The following symptom validity tests may be useful in examining testing effort.

1. Test of Memory Malingering (Tombaugh, 1996).
2. Word Memory Test (Green, 2003).
3. Medical Symptom Validity Test (Green, 2004).
4. Validity Indicator Profile (Frederick, 2003).

Intellectual Functioning: An examination of the child's intellectual abilities may be of interest when examining ADHD. Understanding the child's intellectual abilities is also important in understanding other neuropsychological data. This data provides a general comparison point for one's expected range of functioning. Most instruments assessing intellectual functioning have embedded attentional and processing speed measures. Data stemming from such subtests can provide valuable information regarding aspects of such cognitive abilities. Intellectual exam is necessary when determining the presence of a possible comorbid Specific Learning Disorder. Such data may also be helpful when examining a range of other potential comorbid conditions.

The following are examples of some commonly administered tests when the child's intellectual functioning is of interest.

1. Wechsler Intelligence Scale for Children-V (Wechsler, 2014).
2. Wechsler Adult Intelligence Scale, Fourth Edition (Wechsler, 2008).
3. Wechsler Abbreviated Scale of Intelligence, Second Edition (Wechsler, 2011).
4. Wechsler Preschool and Primary Scale of Intelligence, Fourth Edition (Wechsler, 2012).
5. Woodcock-Johnson IV Tests of Cognitive Abilities (Schrank, McGrew, & Mather, 2014).
6. Differential Abilities Scales, Second Edition (DAS-II) (Elliott, 2006).
7. Kaufman Assessment Battery for Children, Second Edition (Kaufman & Kaufman, 2004).
8. Reynolds Intellectual Assessment Scales, Second Edition (Reynolds & Kamphaus, 2015).
9. Stanford-Binet Intelligence Scales, Fifth Edition (Roid, 2003).

Attention: Attentional measures are important to administer in any neuropsychological battery when the goal is to determine whether or not ADHD is present. Such measures can provide valuable data to inform the psychologist of various attentional processes. These include aspects of focused attention, sustained attention, divided attention, and working memory.

Focused or *selective attention* refers to active concentration on specific stimuli to the exclusion of others. *Sustained attention* refers to one's capacity to focus their attention on a task for an extended period of time. *Divided attention* refers to attentional processes of two or more stimuli at the same time to the extent that two or more tasks may be performed simultaneously. Divided attention is important in multitasking. *Working memory* is a cognitive process that involves the short-term maintenance of information along with the ability to manipulate and process such information. Working memory processes are important in learning new information, transferring it to longer-term memory, comprehension, and reasoning.

Continuous Performance Tests (CPT) are often helpful measures to administer in an ADHD neuropsychological test battery. Such tests typically measure sustained and focused attention. Some involve components that also examine aspects of information-processing speed and impulsivity. Such tests usually require the child to respond to auditory or visual targets stimuli while ignoring nontarget stimuli.

The *Connors Continuous Performance Test-II* (Conners, 2004) and the recently published *Conners Continuous Performance Test 3* (Conners CPT-3; Conners, 2014) are continuous performance tests that examine aspects of visual focused attention, sustained attention, and impulsivity. Both tests are 14 minutes in length. The Conners Continuous Performance Test-II allows for unlimited test administrations. The Conners Continuous Performance Test 3 may be purchased per test administration or for unlimited use. Both of these instruments are computer administered.

The *Conners Continuous Auditory Test of Attention* (Conners, 2014) is a computer-based continuous performance test that examines auditory processing and auditory attentional processes. This measure provides information regarding a patient's auditory focused attention, sustained attention, and impulsivity. This instrument also yields information regarding a child's auditory laterality (i.e., preference for left vs. right targets) and auditory mobility (i.e., ability to switch attention from one ear to the other). Norms are available for ages 8 to 60+ years. The Conners CATA can be purchased as unlimited use or pay per use. Test administration is 14 minutes in length. All of these instruments are available from MHS (www.mhs.com).

The *Test of Variables of Attention (TOVA*; Leark, Greenberg, Kindschi, Dupuy, & Hughes, 2007) is another continuous performance test that can be useful in the evaluation of ADHD. The TOVA examines aspects of selective attention, sustained attention, and impulsivity. The TOVA is computer administered. The TOVA involves separate tests examining aspects of visual and auditory attention. Both age and gender norm options are available for both the visual and auditory components of this instrument. The visual component of the TOVA is normed for ages 4 to 80+ years. The auditory TOVA test has norms for ages 6 to 29+ years. The length of the test administration is 10.9 minutes for children ages 4 and 5 years, and 21.8 minutes for persons who are age 6+ years. Administering the TOVA requires purchase of the TOVA software along with a fee per test administration. The TOVA is available via the TOVA Company (www.tovatest.com).

The *Intermediate Visual & Auditory Continuous Performance Test (IVA+plus/IVA-2*; Sandford & Turner, 2004) is a computer-based CPT that is helpful in the assessment of ADHD. As with other CPT instruments, the IVA examines focused attention, sustained attention, and impulsivity. This instrument allows for the examination of both auditory and visual attentional processes. Normative data is available for ages 6 to 96 years. Test administration is 15 minutes. The IVA-2 and IVA+Plus test procedures and structures are the same. The difference between the two tests is that the IVA-2 includes a more detailed interpretative report, it integrates ADHD rating scale data in the interpretative analysis, and it has an enhanced modern user interface. The IVA-2 also has an improved malingering analysis and interpretation, built-in report word processor, researcher tool kit, and an improved working diagnosis flowchart. The IVA-2 can be purchased from BrainTrain (www.braintrain.com). Purchase options include pay per test administration, unlimited test administration, pay per interpretative report, and unlimited interpretative reports.

NEPSY-II (Korkman, Kirk, & Kemp, 2007)*; Auditory Attention and Response Set*—The NEPSY-II is a neuropsychological battery of tests that are appropriate for children ages 3 years through 16 years 11 months. Within this battery are specific subtests that are helpful in examining aspects of attention and other executive abilities. The Auditory Attention and Response Set subtest can provide valuable data when ADHD is the construct of interest. The Auditory Attention and Response Set subtest employs an auditory continuous performance paradigm. This subtest measures selective and sustained auditory attention, response inhibition, and some other aspects of executive functioning. The auditory attention component examines focused auditory attention. The NEPSY-II is available from Pearson Assessments (www.pearsonassessments.com).

A number of other stand=alone tests may be helpful in examining attentional processes. Some other instruments contain subtests that may also be useful in this process. The following is a brief list of instruments that may be considered in the assessment of ADHD.

Brief Test of Attention (BTA; Schretlen, 1997). The BTA assesses auditory divided attention. Test administration is approximately 10 minutes. The test manual lists norms for ages 17 to 82 years, but additional norms are available for children ages 6 to 14 years. The BTA is available from PAR (www.4parinc.com; 800-331-8378).

Paced Auditory Serial Addition Test (PASAT; Diehr, Heaton, Miller, & Grant, 1998; Gronwall, 1977) and *Children's Paced Auditory Serial Addition Test* (CHIPASAT; Johnson, Roethig-Johnson, & Middleton, 1988). The PASAT and CHIPASAT assess auditory working memory, sustained attention, divided attention, and information-processing speed. Administration time is approximately 15 to 20 minutes for each test. The PASAT is normed for ages 16 to 74 years. The CHIPASAT is normed for ages 8 to 14 years. Computerized versions of the PASAT and CHIPASAT are available for purchase from Robert J. McInerney, PhD (www.Robert McInerney.ca).

Test of Everyday Attention for Children (TEA-Ch; Manly, Robertson, Anderson, & Nimmo-Smith, 1999). The TEA-Ch is a battery of nine tasks that measure aspects of focused attention, sustained attention, divided attention, attentional control/switching, and inhibition. Test administration time is approximately 1 hour. The TEA-Ch is normed for children age 6 to 16 years. It is available from Pearson Assessments (www. pearsonassessments.com; 800-328-5999).

Stroop Color and Word Test (Golden & Freshwater, 2002; Golden, Freshwater, & Golden, 2003). The Stroop Color and Word Test assesses selective attention, cognitive flexibility, and response inhibition. The Stroop test was originally developed by Stroop (1935). Several versions of the Stroop paradigm are in circulation and commercially available. This includes the Stroop Color and Word Test by Charles Golden and colleagues. Administration time is approximately 5 to 10 minutes. Golden's Stroop Color and Word Test is available from PAR (www4.parinc.com; 800-331-8378) in two versions—for children (ages 5 to 14 years) and for older adolescents/adults (ages 15 to 90 years).

Trail-Making Tests. Tests employing the trail-making paradigm are commercially available in various forms. These tests generally examine focused attention, sustained attention, sequencing, and cognitive flexibility. Examples include the *Comprehensive Trail-Making Test* (CTMT; Reynolds, 2002); *Children's Color Trails Test* (CCTT; Llorente, Williams, Satz, & D'Elia, 2003); *Trail Making Test, Parts A & B* (Reitan, 1955; Reitan & Wolfson, 2004); and the *Trail Making Test* from the *Delis-Kaplan Executive Function System (D-KEFS)* test battery (Delis, Kaplan, & Kramer, 2001).

Wechsler Intelligence Scale for Children—Fifth Edition (WISC-V; Wechsler, 2014). A measure examining a child's intellectual abilities is commonly given in a battery of tests examining ADHD. The WISC-V is one such instrument that is often employed. The WISC-V yields information regarding aspects of a child's attentional processes in addition to their intellectual abilities. The Working Memory Index and Auditory Working Memory Index provide information regarding focused attention and working memory. The Processing Speed Index and Cognitive Proficiency Index provide information regarding speed of cognitive processing abilities. The WISC-V is available from Pearson Assessments (www.pearsonassessment.com; 800-328-5999).

Executive Functions: Attentional abilities are one aspect of executive functioning. Executive functions also involve a range of other cognitive processes, including planning, organization, problem solving, reasoning, applying logic, behavioral initiation, inhibition of impulses, concept formation, and cognitive flexibility. ADHD can be conceptualized as a spectrum disorder involving impaired executive abilities. Such impairments are often over and above attentional deficits. Evaluating such competing executive abilities may be helpful in identifying ADHD along with providing an understanding of specific executive deficits that are demonstrated. A detailed understanding of a child's executive deficits can sometimes assist in informing psychological, educational, and other (e.g., executive coaching) treatment planning.

The following neuropsychological tests are examples of instruments that examine different aspects of one's executive abilities.

1. Delis-Kaplan Executive Function System (Delis, Kaplan, & Kramer, 2001)
2. Kaufman Assessment Battery for Children-II (Kaufman & Kaufman, 2004); Pattern Reasoning, Story Completion, Rover
3. Reynolds Intellectual Assessment Scales, Second Edition (Reynolds & Kamphaus, 2015); Guess What, Odd-Item Out, Verbal Reasoning
4. NEPSY-II (Korkman, Kirk, & Kemp, 2007); Animal Sorting, Clocks, Design Fluency, Inhibition, Statue, Word Generation
5. WPPSI-IV (Wechsler, 2012), WISC-V (Wechsler, 2014), WAIS-IV (Wechsler, 2008), WASI-II (Wechsler, 2011); Similarities, Matrix Reasoning
6. Woodcock—Johnson IV Cognitive Battery (Schrank, McGrew, & Mather, 2014); Analysis-Synthesis, Concept Formation, Number Series
7. Wisconsin Card Sorting Test (Heaton, Chelune, Talley, Kay, & Curtis, 1993)

A limitation of neuropsychological tests is that many do not examine other important aspects of frontal-lobe functioning. Examples include behavioral initiation, motivation, inhibiting one's impulses, emotional control, goal-directed behavior, sense of time, and insight. Parent-reported measures involving ratings of their child's executive functioning are often important to include in an ADHD test battery in order to gain an understanding of these executive skills. Listed as follows are examples of such self-report instruments.

- Barkley Deficits in Executive Functioning Scale—Child & Adolescent (Barkley, 2012)
- Behavior Rating Inventory of Executive Function, Second Edition (Gioia, Isquith, Guy, & Kenworthy, 2015)
- Delis Rating of Executive Function (Delis, 2012)

Language Functioning: Evaluating a child's ability to communicate may be of interest in neuropsychological examination. Examining aspects of expressive and receptive language functions should be considered when a communication disorder and/or language-based learning disorder are suspected. Communication disorders in children are discussed in a different book in the series. Briefly, such communication disorders refer to specific difficulties with speech and language. Such disorders may take the form of difficulties with expressive language (e.g., reduced word knowledge and use, difficulty producing complete sentences, problems recalling words, impairments in discourse, articulation difficulties, stuttering). Difficulties with receptive language (e.g., auditory processing, complex auditory comprehension, difficulties understanding what is not explicitly stated, problems in making inferences) may also be of concern. It is possible for persons to demonstrate some combination of both expressive and receptive language difficulties. Such language delays can result in a range of functional impairments in relation to the child's academic functioning, social interactions, relationships, participation in activities, work performance, and their general ability to effectively communicate with others.

The following are some neuropsychological tests that could be considered when concerns of possible expressive and/or receptive language delays have been raised:

- WPPSI-IV (Wechsler, 2012), WISC-V (Wechsler, 2014), WAIS-IV (Wechsler, 2008), WASI-II (Wechsler, 2011); Vocabulary, Similarities
- NESPY-II (Korkman, Kirk, & Kemp, 2007); Comprehension of Instructions, Phonological Processing, Speeded Naming, Repetition of Nonsense Words, Word Generation
- D-KEFS (Delis, Kaplan, & Kramer, 2001); Verbal Fluency Test

- Woodcock-Johnson IV Test of Cognitive Abilities (Schrank, McGrew, & Mather, 2014); Oral Vocabulary, Oral Comprehension, Phonological Processing
- Comprehensive Test of Phonological Processing-2 (Wagner, Torgesen, Rashotte, & Pearson, 2013)
- Reynolds Intellectual Assessment Scales-2 (Reynolds & Kamphaus, 2015); Verbal Reasoning
- Clinical Evaluation of Language Fundamentals, Fifth Edition (Wiig, Semel, & Secord, 2013).
- Test of Auditory Processing Skills, Third Edition (TAPS-3; Martin & Brownell, 2005)
- Kaufman Test of Educational Achievement, Third Edition (Kaufman & Kaufaman, 2014)
- Test of Language Development–Intermediate, Fourth Edition (Hammill & Newcomer, 2008)
- Kaufman Assessment Battery for Children-II (Kaufman & Kaufman, 2004); Verbal Knowledge, Riddles

Visuospatial skills: Visuospatial skills refer to one's ability to perceive the spatial aspects of a figure or object in two and three dimensions. Potential visual-spatial deficits are important to explore especially when the purpose of the exam includes ruling out potential dyslexia, dysgraphia, dyscalculia, or a Nonverbal Learning Disorder. Some variants of these learning disorders are due to specific visual-spatial deficits. This is discussed in more detail in one of the other books that comprise this book series. The following neuropsychological tasks may be helpful in understanding a child's visual-spatial functions.

- Beery-Buktenica Developmental Test of Visual-Motor Integration, Sixth Edition (Beery, Buktenica, & Beery, 2010)
- Beery-Buktenica Developmental Test of Visual-Perception, Sixth Edition (Beery, Buktenica, & Beery, 2010)
- Rey Complex Figure Test and Recognition Trial (Meyers & Meyers, 1995)
- Test of Visual-Perception Skills, Third Edition (Martin, 2006)
- Benton Judgment of Line Orientation (Benton et al., 1994)

- Differential Abilities Scales, Second Edition (Elliott, 2006); Copying, Matching Letter-Like Forms, Pattern Construction

1. Kaufman Assessment Battery for Children, Second Edition (Kaufman & Kaufman, 2004); Block Counting, Triangles
   - NEPSY-II (Korkman, Kirk, & Kemp, 2007); Arrows, Block Construction, Design Copying
   - WISC-V (Wechsler, 2014); Block Design, Visual Puzzles
   - WAIS-IV (Wechsler, 2008) & WASI-II (Wechsler, 2011); Block Design
   - WJ-III Tests of Cognitive Abilities (Schrank, McGrew, & Mather, 2014); Visualization

Memory: Memory refers to the process by which an individual encodes, stores, and retrieves information. An examination of the child's memory abilities may be of interest when examining children and adolescents with suspected ADHD. The following are some examples of instruments that could be considered when objective assessment of memory abilities is a goal of exam.

- NEPSY-II (Korkman, Kirk, & Kemp, 2007); Narrative Memory, List Memory, Memory for Faces, Memory for Designs, Memory for Names
- Children's Memory Scale (Cohen, 1997)
- Wide Range Assessment of Memory and Learning, Second Edition (Sheslow & Adams, 2003)
- California Verbal Learning Test—Children's Version (Delis, Kramer, Kaplan, & Ober, 1994)
- Reynolds Intellectual Assessment Scales, Second Edition (Reynolds & Kamphaus, 2015); Verbal Memory, Nonverbal Memory
- Test of Memory and Learning, Second Edition (Reynolds & Voress, 2007)

Motor functions: A percentage of children and adolescents demonstrating ADHD display concurrent fine-motor-coordination deficits.

Such challenges may negatively impact their learning experiences and academic performance given difficulties with the speed and/or quality of their handwriting. Difficulties in fine motor coordination may negatively impact a child's participation in sports or other leisure activities. Some of these difficulties may also negatively affect the child's independent-living skills, such as learning how to tie shoelaces and performing other tasks that require such abilities (e.g., doing zippers or buttons). The following instruments may be helpful when examining the possibility of delays in fine motor coordination.

- Finger Tapping Test (Reitan, 1969)
- Grooved Pegboard Test (Matthews & Klove, 1964)
- Purdue Pegboard Test (Matthews & Klove, 1964; Gardner & Brinab, 1979)
- Beery-Buktenica Developmental Test of Motor Coordination, Sixth Edition (Beery, Buktenica, & Beery, 2010)
- NEPSY-II (Korkman, Kirk, & Kemp, 2007); Fingertip Tapping, Visuomotor Precision
- Dean-Woodcock Neuropsychological Battery (Dean & Woodcock, 2003)

Academic Achievement: There is a relatively high rate of comorbidity between Specific Learning Disorders and ADHD. Ruling out a coexisting learning disorder may be a goal of assessment when the child's developmental history suggests possible learning delays.

It is important to administer a comprehensive-achievement test battery (e.g., WIAT-III, WJ-IV) when determining if a specific learning disorder is present. Such a battery may be supplemented by additional tests (e.g., GORT-5, CTOPP-2) depending on the construct of interest. Administration of a screening battery (e.g., WRAT-4) does not suffice when the goal is to rule out a specific learning disability. The following achievement and other neuropsychological tests may be of interest when a specific learning disorder is suspected.

- Weschsler Individual Achievement Test, Third Edition (Wechsler, 2009)

- Woodcock-Johnson Tests of Achievement, Fourth Edition (Schrank, Mather, & McGrew, 2014)
- Wide Range Achievement Test, Fourth Edition (WRAT-4) (Wilkinson & Robertson, 2006)
- Kaufman Test of Educational Achievement, Third Edition (Kaufman & Kaufman, 2014)
- Gray Oral Reading Tests, Fifth Edition (GORT-5) (Wiederholt & Bryant, 2012)
- Comprehensive Test of Phonological Processing, Second Edition (Wagner, Torgesen, Rashotte, & Pearson, 2013)
- NEPSY-II (Korkman, Kirk, & Kemp, 2007); Phonological Processing, Repetition of Nonsense Words, Speeded Naming, Design Copying

Feedback Session and Treatment Planning

The final phase in the ADHD assessment is to provide feedback to parents and the child who was examined. This is very important so that all persons understand the diagnosis of ADHD, test results, other important examination findings, and interventions to be pursued. I generally include adolescents in the entire feedback session. I may possibly talk to their parents alone for a short time if there is some information that needs to be communicated that I believe would not be in the child's best interest to hear. I usually provide feedback to parents alone for child exams, yet will invite the child into the session at the end to provide them with a basic explanation of the evaluation results. For young children (i.e., age 7 years and younger) I usually tell the parents that bringing the child to the feedback session is optional. This format is simply a stylistic perspective and other psychologists may have other methods to provide children and their parents with feedback regarding examination results.

An effective feedback in many ways is like a well-written journal article. By the time someone reaches the Discussion section, the conclusions are quite obvious. Providing information in a direct and concise manner is highly preferred. One should generally avoid complicated terminology during the feedback process.

I generally start the feedback session by briefly reviewing the DSM-5 diagnostic criteria for ADHD. I indicate that there are 18 symptoms of interest, 9 of which pertain to inattention and 9 reflect hyperactivity and impulsivity. I note that one needs to display a minimum of 6 out of 9 symptoms of ADHD-related Inattention and/or 6 out of 9 symptoms of ADHD-related Hyperactivity/Impulsivity in order to possibly qualify for this diagnosis. I review the number of symptoms that the parent, and possibly the child, reported per the structured clinical interview that had been administered at the intake session. I state the number of ADHD-related symptoms that were endorsed by each person. I then review behavior checklists that were completed by the parent, teachers, and the child as applicable. I typically give a brief explanation of the psychometric properties associated with each instrument (e.g., scores at the 95th percentile and above are significant). I will review all pertinent scale elevations illustrating data that is either consistent with ADHD or not. I will also typically concurrently provide feedback regarding other concerns (e.g., behavioral disturbances, depression, anxiety) that each rater communicated per such measures.

I will walk the parents and child through the neuropsychological data if such instruments were administered as part of the test battery. I usually start by providing a brief and basic explanation of how these tests were normed. I note that such tests objectively measure brain functioning (e.g., attention/concentration, memory, processing speed) and explain how the scores work. I then briefly review the results of each test. I believe that it is important to point out specific strengths, and not just weaknesses or deficits, in this process.

I will offer my opinions once all data has been reviewed. I believe that it is important to be direct about assessment results. The evaluating psychologist or physician is doing a disservice by sugarcoating the issues that need to be communicated. I specifically state why I believe that the child being examined demonstrates a diagnosis of ADHD, including what variant of ADHD he or she displays. Alternatively, I will state why I do not believe that the child truly displays ADHD when none seems apparent. I will also offer an opinion regarding other diagnoses (e.g., a Specific Learning Disorder, comorbid psychological disorders) as appropriate. I then launch into some brief education regarding ADHD. I emphasize that

ADHD is a biologically based neurodevelopmental condition. It is not a mental illness or psychologically based disorder. Equally, ADHD is not being of substandard intellect or lazy, or a reflection of poor parenting.

Finally, I will offer an opinion regarding other issues that may be pertinent to address in the treatment plan. For example, if a parent is suspected of demonstrating an untreated Attention-Deficit/Hyperactivity Disorder of their own, I will provide education regarding research that has demonstrated that treating parents who display ADHD is an important part of the child's treatment plan. Other points of discussion may include the child's academic effort, parenting styles, or other pertinent psychosocial issues. I usually stop the feedback session at this point, check for understanding, and ask if parents or the child have any questions regarding the results that were communicated.

The next part of the feedback session involves discussing treatment planning. This usually begins with providing education regarding effective treatment options for ADHD (e.g., medication, behavioral training for parents, implementing behavior modification techniques). At the time of this publication, few psychologists in the United States have prescription privileges. I am one of the majority of psychologists who are not licensed to prescribe medication. I believe that psychologists who provide ADHD assessments and treatment should be well versed in medication interventions for ADHD. As such, I provide parents and the child with education regarding medication options. If it is my opinion that the child may benefit from pharmacological interventions, then I communicate this directly in the feedback session. I point out that I am unable to prescribe medication due to my licensure. I note that they should follow up with the child's physician to discuss medication options in light of the current test results. Parents should do the same with a psychiatrist if the child would be better served in such a capacity. I will typically review some examples of behavior modification strategies that may be helpful to implement. This may include the development of a 504 Plan or Individualized Education Program at school and strategies to employ at home. I typically provide parents some psychoeducational handouts regarding behavior modification strategies and information regarding ADHD.

The feedback session also includes a discussion of other treatments and interventions that may be necessary given the child's issues. Such interventions typically address the specific concerns that relate to any accompanying comorbid conditions that are displayed (e.g., Specific Learning Disorder, Developmental Coordination Disorder, psychological disorder). Examples of interventions may include psychological therapy, speech therapy, occupational therapy, specialized tutoring (e.g., Orton-Gillingham interventions), using technology, and whatever else is appropriate. I usually ask parents at the feedback session if they would like me to facilitate such referrals. Parents are typically grateful that such an offer has been extended. I have parents sign appropriate releases of information as needed at the feedback session. I then ask the child and parents if they have any questions regarding anything covered in the feedback session. Such a feedback session usually takes around 60 minutes to complete.

The follow-up plan is a very important part of the assessment procedure. I believe that it is paramount for the evaluator to assist in facilitating linkage with whatever necessary services may be needed. This usually entails the psychologist providing a direct referral to any necessary follow-up treatment providers. For any referrals, I like to provide detailed information regarding the purpose of treatment, what concerns need to be targeted, and sometimes specific recommendations regarding techniques. The results of the evaluation directly guide these referral recommendations.

It is important to provide follow-up treatment providers with all pertinent information. This includes a copy of the assessment report, contact information, insurance information, and specific reason for referral. The art of writing a good referral seems to have gone the wayside in recent years, especially with the pressures of managed care and use of electronic medical records. Nonetheless, spending a few extra minutes and writing a more detailed referral can often make a big difference in the child's treatment.

The Written Report

A written report is the final product of an ADHD assessment. I believe that it is important that parents receive a copy of the written report. The written report should also be sent to the referring provider and any follow-up treatment providers. I usually send parents the report that is issued to other providers. A good report should generally be easy for the consumer to understand, although some reports may require medical and other technical information that is meant specifically for physicians, psychologists, or other treatment providers.

Reports should be clear and concise. Reports should include appropriate demographic information, examination dates, and a listing of tests/procedures that were employed. The report should communicate why the exam was conducted. Reports should typically include a description of presenting symptoms and behaviors of concern, other symptoms as appropriate, developmental history, medical history, psychiatric/psychological history, family history, educational history, and other relevant psychosocial history. Reports may include behavior observations or mental status examination. The results of any tests that were administered should be outlined. Interpretations of these tests should be offered. Listing the actual data may depend on the purpose of the exam. For example, listing all scores may be important for educational planning. Most school districts require such information. Specific diagnoses should be offered. The report should include a rationale of how the examiner reached their conclusions. Finally, recommendations for treatment and other interventions as needed should be communicated. Some examples of reports are offered in Chapter 5 of this book.

CHAPTER 4

Treatment of Attention-Deficit/Hyperactivity Disorders

Why should children and adolescents who demonstrate ADHD pursue treatment? This question is sometimes asked by parents whose child demonstrates ADHD. Some parents are hesitant to have their child pursue treatment for ADHD, especially medication, for a variety of reasons. Others are sometimes concerned that their child is labeled with such a diagnosis. Therefore, providing education to parents and children regarding ADHD and the potential benefits of treatment is usually the first step in the treatment process.

Providing parents with education about the possible effects of untreated ADHD may also potentially increase the likelihood that treatments are pursued. Untreated ADHD can result in a number of negative outcomes. Academic underachievement and/or failure occur for many children who display ADHD. Untreated ADHD may have a significant negative impact on the child's academic performance. This is often expressed in poor study habits, limited to no study, poor grades, procrastination, suboptimal effort, lost homework, and incomplete or missed assignments. Such behavior can have a deleterious effect on the child's academic grades. For some children, such academic difficulties may be less apparent. At face value, they may be receiving reasonably good grades and completing the necessary work. However, they may have to put forth incredible efforts (e.g., devoting excessive hours to study or assignment completion) in order to achieve at this level. Others may be doing reasonably well academically but are underachieving.

Untreated ADHD often directly relates to a range of disruptive behaviors that are displayed by a larger proportion of children and adolescents who display this condition. These include a range of oppositional and antisocial behaviors associated with DSM-5 diagnoses of Oppositional Defiant Disorder and Conduct Disorder. In turn, such disruptive behavior may negatively impact the child's learning experiences at school, peer relationships, friendships, and functioning within the family. It is often paramount to treat ADHD in order to gain better control of such behavior.

Untreated ADHD can relate to a number of other difficulties for the child or adolescent. This may include suboptimal performance in sports or other recreational activities. Difficulties may extend to the completion of various tasks, performance in a part-time job, driving a motor vehicle, poor decision making, engaging in reckless behaviors, and managing other aspects of their day-to-day activities.

The International Consensus Statement on ADHD (Barkley et al., 2002) points out that ADHD is not a benign condition. Persons with ADHD are more likely to experience a range of problems and other difficulties as compared to individuals who do not demonstrate this condition. Educational problems are common. As compared to persons without ADHD, research indicates that 32 to 40 percent drop out of school, and few complete college (5 to 10 percent). A large number of persons with ADHD engage in antisocial activities (40 to 50 percent), and substance abuse problems are more common. Teenage pregnancy is experienced at a much higher rate (40 percent) as are sexually transmitted diseases (16 percent). Persons with ADHD are more likely to experience depression (20 to 30 percent) and personality disorders as adults (18 to 25 percent). The International Consensus Statement on ADHD is a good article to provide to parents who are hesitant to address their child's ADHD-related concerns.

Research indicates that specific treatments can be helpful in treating children and adolescents who demonstrate an Attention-Deficit/Hyperactivity Disorder. The efficacy of such interventions varies, and the combination of more than one intervention is often the most helpful. Interventions that have demonstrated efficacy in treating ADHD include stimulant and nonstimulant medications, behavioral parent training, and behavioral interventions in the classroom. Treating comorbid conditions (e.g., a Specific Learning Disorder, psychological disorders) is often paramount in the treatment plan for such children. This chapter discusses different treatment modalities for children and adolescents who demonstrate an Attention-Deficit/Hyperactivity Disorder.

Pharmacological Interventions

Most medication trials examining the efficacy of pharmacological interventions in the treatment of ADHD typically involve a double-blind controlled treatment outcome study pitting the experimental drug against a placebo. The large majority of these studies employ statistics exploring whether or not there are statistically significant discrepancies between the treatment and control groups on a range of outcome measures. To date, there is overwhelming evidence indicating that a number of stimulant (i.e., amphetamines, methylphenidates) and nonstimulant (e.g., atomoxetine, extended-release a_2-adrenergic agonists) medications outperform placebo in the treatment of ADHD in children and adolescents (e.g., Chan, Fogler, & Hammermess, 2016; Faraone, 2009; MTA Cooperative Group, 1999; Tanaka, Rohde, Jin, Fieldman & Upadhyaya, 2013; Wilens et al., 2015). Commonly prescribed stimulant and nonstimulant medications for ADHD are presented in the following tables.

Short-Acting Amphetamine

Trade Name	Compound/Generic Name	FDA-approved Age (Children)
Adderall	mixed amphetamine salts	≥ 3 years old
Dexedrine	dextroamphetamine	≥ 3 years old
Dextrostat	dextroamphetamine	≥ 6 years old
Procentra	dextroamphetamine	≥ 3 years old
Zenzedi	dextroamphetamine	≥ 3 years old
Evekeo	amphetamine	≥ 3 years old

Long-Acting Amphetamine

Trade Name	Compound/Generic Name	FDA-Approved Age (Children)
Adderall XR	mixed amphetamine salts extended release	$\geq$ 6 years old
Dexedrine Spansule	dextroamphetamine sulfate	$\geq$ 6 years old
Vyvanse	lisdexamfetamine	$\geq$ 6 years old
Adzenys XR-ODT	amphetamine extended release	$\geq$ 6 years old
Dyanavel XR	amphetamine extended release (liquid)	$\geq$ 6 years old
MYDAYIS	mixed amphetamine salts extended release	$\geq$ 13 years old

Short-Acting Methylphenidate

Trade Name	Compound/Generic Name	FDA-Approved Age
Ritalin	methylphenidate	children > 6 years old
Focalin	dexmethylphenidate	children $\geq$ 6 years old
Methylin	methylphenidate	children $\geq$ 6 years old

Mid- to Long-Acting Methylphenidate

Trade Name	Compound/Generic Name	FDA-Approved Age
Metadate CD	methylphenidate extended release	children $\geq$ 6 years old
Metadate ER	methylphenidate extended release	children $\geq$ 6 years old
Ritalin SR	methylphenidate extended release	children $\geq$ 6 years old
Ritalin LA	methylphenidate extended release	children $\geq$ 6 years old
Methylin ER	methylphenidate extended release	children $\geq$ 6 years old
Concerta	methylphenidate extended release	children $\geq$ 6 years old

Trade Name	Compound/Generic Name	FDA-Approved Age
Quillivant XR	methylphenidate extended release (liquid)	children $\geq$ 6 years old
Quillichew ER	methylphenidate extended release (chewable)	children $\geq$ 6 years old
Focalin XR	dexmethylphenidate extended release	children $\geq$ 6 years old
Daytrana Patch	methylphenidate extended release (adhesive patch)	children $\geq$ 6 years old
Aptensio XR	methylphenidate extended release	children $\geq$ 6 years old

Nonstimulant Medications

Trade Name	Compound/Generic Name	FDA-Approved Age
Strattera	atomoxetine	children $\geq$ 6 years old
Intuniv	guanfacine extended release	children $\geq$ 6 years old
Kapvay	clonidine extended release	children $\geq$ 6 years old

Psychostimulant Medication

Psychostimulant agents are typically the first line of medication management for children and adolescents demonstrating ADHD. These medications include compounds of methylphenidate or amphetamine. Stimulant medications generally enhance dopaminergic and noradrenergic neurotransmission in the central nervous system. Both methylphenidate- and amphetamine—based medications block the reuptake transporter and increase the output so that more dopamine and norepinephrine are available in the synapse. Research indicates that between 65 and 75 percent of children with ADHD who are treated with psychostimulant medication experience significant reduction of symptoms. Approximately 25 to 30 percent of these children do not respond or cannot tolerate the initial stimulant medication that is prescribed. However, approximately 80 to 90 percent respond if a second psychostimulant trial is pursued (Pliszka, 2007).

Stimulant medications are associated with potential side effects. Common side effects include decreased appetite, insomnia, headache, stomachache, and small increases in heart rate and blood pressure. Higher doses of psychostimulant medication are typically associated with more reported side effects. The use of stimulant medication may possibly exacerbate tics for children who demonstrate Tourette's or other Tic Disorder. Such medication can also exacerbate symptoms of psychosis for persons who demonstrate a schizophrenic illness or bipolar disorder. Psychosis can also be an acute manifestation of stimulant toxicity. Long-term side effects include potential negative effects on weight and height, especially for children ages 12 years and younger (Faraone, Biederman, Morley, & Spencer, 2008). Therefore, standards of practice necessitate monitoring the child's height, weight, and body mass index for gender and age. A clinical response (e.g., changing medication, dose reduction, drug holiday) from the prescribing physician is needed if there is a change in weight or height crossing two percentile lines on a standardized growth curve.

Both amphetamine and methylphenidate medications have black box warnings in their package inserts. Amphetamine is cautioned as having a high abuse potential. Serious cardiovascular adverse events and sudden death have been reported with misuse of this medication. The black box warnings for methylphenidate include potential dependence and psychosis. Careful supervision is advised during withdrawal given that discontinuation may unmask depression or effects of chronic overactivity. Further, basic personality disturbances may require long-term follow-up.

Methylphenidate

Methylphenidate is the oldest agent approved for the treatment of ADHD. It was approved by the FDA more than 60 years ago (i.e., in 1955) for ADHD treatment. Methylphenidate medications are available in both shorter- and longer-acting compounds, as outlined in the previous tables. Methylphenidate is thought to inhibit the reuptake of dopamine, and to a lesser extent norepinephrine, into presynaptic neurons. This results in increased sympathomimetic activity in the central nervous system. In turn, this typically relates to improvements in attentional processes along with decreased overactivity and impulsivity.

Methylphenidate is available in the form of tablet, chewable tablet, capsule, liquid solution, and transdermal patch. Chewable tablets (e.g., Quillichew ER), oral solutions (e.g., Quillivant XR), and adhesive patch (i.e., Daytrana patch) are appealing options for children who are unable to swallow pills. Immediate-release methylphenidate tablets can be crushed and added to food. Most extended-release methylphenidate preparations (e.g., Concerta, Medadate ER, Ritalin SR) cannot be crushed due to the nature of their delivery system. These medications must be swallowed whole.

Decreased appetite and weight loss are potential side effects of methylphenidate. This should especially be closely monitored in children 12 years and under. Other potential side effects of methylphenidate include headache, insomnia, nausea, dizziness, irritability, stomachache, exacerbation of tics, anxiety, and mild increase in blood pressure level and pulse. Studies employing the Daytrana patch have noted complaints of localized skin irritation for some persons.

Amphetamine

Mixed amphetamine salts were first approved by the FDA for the treatment of ADHD in 1994, although amphetamine agents date back to the 1930s. Amphetamine is thought to increase the release of dopamine and norepinephrine while inhibiting their reuptake. At higher doses amphetamine can stimulate the release of serotonin. The nature of amphetamine's mechanism of action can also sometimes result in decreased fatigue and increased positive feelings. These effects on the central nervous system are the mechanisms that relate to decreases of symptoms associated with ADHD.

Amphetamine is available in tablet (e.g., Adderall, Eveko), capsule (e.g., Adderall XR), and liquid (i.e., Dyanavel XR) formats. Adzenys is an orally disintegrating amphetamine tablet.

Amphetamine is available in both short- and extended-release formulations. The instant release forms of amphetamine can be crushed and taken with food (e.g., applesauce). Extended-release agents (e.g., Adderall XR, Vyvanse, Mydayis) should be taken whole, but the capsule may be opened and the contents taken with food if the child is unable to swallow the pill. Care must be taken to ensure that the child ingests all contents of the opened capsule as the extended-release beads contained within are not all the same.

Lisdexamfetamine (Vyvanse) is somewhat of a qualitatively different amphetamine-based medication. It is a pharmacologically inactive pro-drug that is comprised of the amino acid L-lysine covalently bound to dextroamphetamine. Lisdexamfetamine is rapidly absorbed from the gastrointestinal tract after ingestion. Lisdexamfetamine is converted to dextroamphetamine and L-lysine primarily in the blood due to the hydrolytic activity of red blood cells. An advantage of lisdexamfetamine is a longer duration of action due to its delivery system. Lisdexamfetamine may also be a good option when there are concerns regarding substance abuse. This is because dextroamphetamine is not released until it has been cleaved in the gastrointestinal tract; snorting lisdexamfetamine will not generally lead to the high that can be obtained from snorting crushed amphetamine pills.

MYDAYIS is Shire's newest extended-release amphetamine medication. Its use to treat ADHD in persons 13 years and older was approved by the FDA in 2017. MYDAYIS is a capsule containing equal amounts (by weight) of four amphetamine salts: dextroamphetamine sulfate and amphetamine sulfate, dextroamphetamine saccharate and amphetamine aspartate monohydrate. This combination results in a 3:1 mixture of dextro-to levo-amphetamine base equivalent. A unique feature of MYDAYIS is that its effects may last up to 16 hours.

Potential side effects of amphetamine are similar to those of methylphenidate. Body weight must be carefully monitored given possibilities of anorexia. Other potential side effects include insomnia, exacerbation of tics, anxiety, irritability, headache, irritability, dizziness, upset stomach, increased blood pressure, and increased heart rate.

Nonstimulant Medications

Atomoxetine

Atomoxetine (Strattera) is a nonstimulant medication that was approved by the FDA for the treatment of ADHD in 2002. Atomoxetine is classified as a selective norepinephrine reuptake inhibitor (SNRI). The mechanism of action in atomoxetine is believed to relate to selective inhibition of the presynaptic norepinephrine transporter. Atomoxetine essentially blocks the norepinephrine reuptake inhibitor, increasing the availability of norepinephrine in the synaptic gap.

Atomoxetine must be taken daily. Doses should not be missed, to ensure that blood levels remain within therapeutic limits. Atomoxetine must be swallowed whole. The contents should not be dispersed into a liquid or added to food. This medication may not be a good option for children who cannot swallow pills.

Atomoxetine generally has a lower side-effect profile than the stimulant medications. Potential side effects include upset stomach, decreased appetite, nausea, dizziness, fatigue, increased heart rate, elevated blood pressure, and mood swings. Urinary hesitancy and/or retention can also occur. This may actually be of potential benefit to children who concurrently demonstrate enuresis.

Research indicates that atomoxetine may be efficacious in treating symptoms of ADHD. One must emphasize patience when recommending and prescribing this medication. Atomoxetine must typically be administered for two to four weeks before a response is apparent. Dosing adjustments (e.g., increasing the dose of atomoxetine) may be necessary at that time if ADHD-related symptoms continue to be problematic. It potentially can take a couple of months or longer to find the optimal dose needed for the person who is prescribed atomoxetine. This is in marked contrast to stimulant medications, where a response is immediately apparent shortly after ingestion.

The FDA made a decision to place a black box warning on atomoxetine given that 0.4 percent of children and adolescents who received atomoxetine in the original placebo-controlled trials expressed suicidal ideation. No suicides occurred in these clinical trials. Although this is an extremely low occurrence, patients who are prescribed atomoxetine should be closely monitored given this data.

a_2-Adrenergic Agonists

FDA-approved nonstimulant medication options for children and adolescents with ADHD include the alpha$_2$-receptor agonists. This class includes extended-release guanfacine (Intuniv) and extended-release clonidine (Kapvay). These medications stimulate noradrenergic neurotransmitters in the prefrontal cortex of the brain. Intuniv and Kapvay offer a first-line treatment for ADHD. They can also be used as an alternative for children who did not respond to reasonable stimulant medication trials, for children who could not tolerate stimulant medication, or for those whom stimulants are contraindicated. Both of these medications have been approved by the FDA for monotherapy and as adjuncts to stimulant interventions. They are especially helpful when symptoms of impulsivity are of particular concern.

Intuniv and Kapvay must be swallowed whole. These medications cannot be crushed or chewed. These medications were originally developed to control high blood pressure. Low blood pressure can occur at higher doses. Common side effects of both include fatigue, somnolence, sedation, and dizziness if blood pressure is too low.

Medication for ADHD and the Role of Psychologists

At the time of this publication, very few U.S. states allow psychologists to prescribe medication. The American Psychological Association (APA) supports the movement to gain prescribing rights for psychologists, and qualified psychologists in the states of Iowa, Illinois, Louisiana, and New Mexico are currently able to gain prescription privileges at the time of this publication. Qualified psychologists in the Public Health Service and the U.S. Military as well as those in Guam may also prescribe psychotropic medication. Legislature allowing qualified psychologists prescription privileges is currently being pursued in a number of states.

The purpose of this chapter is not to present arguments in regard to why qualified psychologists should be allowed to prescribe psychotropic medications. Rather, I and others believe that some qualified psychologists can often play an important role in guiding treatment for persons with ADHD, including as it relates to medication management.

In particular, certain areas of the United States have few psychiatrists, and fewer still have Board Certified psychiatrists for children and adolescents. Further, perhaps understandably so, a growing number of psychiatrists in the United States have become increasingly reluctant to accept medical insurance for treatment services rendered, for a variety of reasons. This has left the majority of psychotropic medication management, including medication targeting ADHD, to pediatricians, family practice physicians, and other family practice providers (e.g., physician assistants and nurse practitioners). The majority do an excellent job in this difficult endeavor. However, many have limited training in psychiatry, including child and adolescent psychiatry. This is where many qualified psychologists may provide assistance via education and consultation.

The American Psychological Association developed a set of 17 guidelines for psychologists in regard to their involvement in various pharmacological issues (APA, 2011). These guidelines are outlined in five categories (i.e., General, Education, Assessment, Intervention and Consultation, Relationships) where psychologists may be involved in various pharmacological issues. These guidelines provide excellent ethical and practical recommendations to psychologists who choose to engage in any level of involvement as it relates to a range of pharmacological issues specific to children and adolescents with an Attention-Deficit/Hyperactivity Disorder. These guidelines are as follows.

General

Guideline 1. Psychologists are encouraged to consider objectively the scope of their competence in pharmacotherapy and to seek consultation as appropriate before offering recommendations about psychotropic medications.

Guideline 2. Psychologists are urged to evaluate their own feelings and attitudes about the role of medication in the treatment of psychological disorders, as these feelings and attitudes can potentially affect communications with patients.

Guideline 3. Psychologists involved in prescribing or collaborating are sensitive to the developmental, age and aging, educational, sex and gender, language, health status, and cultural/ethnicity factors that can moderate the interpersonal and biological aspects of pharmacotherapy relevant to the populations they serve.

Education

Guideline 4. Psychologists are urged to identify a level of knowledge concerning pharmacotherapy for the treatment of psychological disorders that is appropriate to the populations they serve and the type of practice they wish to establish and to engage in educational experiences as appropriate to achieve and maintain that level of knowledge.

Guideline 5. Psychologists strive to be sensitive to the potential for adverse effects associated with the psychotropic medications used by their patients.

Guideline 6. Psychologists involved in prescribing or collaborating are encouraged to familiarize themselves with the technological resources that can enhance decision making during the course of treatment.

Assessment

Guideline 7. Psychologists with prescriptive authority strive to familiarize themselves with key procedures for monitoring the physical and psychological sequelae of the medications used to treat psychological disorders, including laboratory examinations and overt signs of adverse or unintended effects.

Guideline 8. Psychologists with prescriptive authority regularly strive to monitor the physiological status of the patients they treat with medication, particularly when there is a physical condition that might complicate the response to psychotropic medication or predispose a patient to experience an adverse reaction.

Guideline 9. Psychologists are encouraged to explore issues surrounding patient adherence and feelings about medication.

Intervention and Consultation

Guideline 10. Psychologists are urged to develop a relationship that will allow the populations they serve to feel comfortable exploring issues surrounding medication use.

Guideline 11. To the extent deemed appropriate, psychologists involved in prescribing or collaboration adapt a biopsychosocial approach to case formulation that considers both psychosocial and biological factors.

Guideline 12. The psychologist with prescriptive authority is encouraged to use an expanded informed consent process to incorporate additional issues specific to prescribing.

Guideline 13. When making decisions about the use of psychological treatments, pharmacotherapy, or their combination, the psychologist with prescriptive authority considers the best interests of the patient, current research, and when appropriate, the needs of the community.

Guideline 14. Psychologists involved in prescribing or collaborating strive to be sensitive to the subtle influences of effective marketing on professional behavior and the potential for bias in information in their clinical decisions about the use of medications.

Guideline 15. Psychologists with prescriptive authority are encouraged to use interactions with the patient surrounding the act of prescribing to learn more about the patient's characteristic patterns of interpersonal behavior.

Relationships

Guideline 16. Psychologists with prescriptive authority are sensitive to maintaining appropriate relationships with other providers of psychological services.

Guideline 17. Psychologists are urged to maintain appropriate relationships with providers of biological interventions.

Behavioral Interventions for ADHD

Behavioral Parent Training (BPT)

Research has demonstrated that parent-administered behavioral interventions are effective interventions for children who demonstrate ADHD. Controlled outcome studies employing such behavioral interventions consistently demonstrate a moderate reduction of children's ADHD symptoms and conduct problems (Chan, Fogler, & Hammerness, 2016; Coates, Taylor, & Sayal, 2014).

Behavioral Parent Training is appropriate for parents of preschool and school-age children. Sessions are structured, typically an hour long, conducted weekly, and involve homework assignments. Most BPT programs involve at least 12 sessions. A number of structured BPT programs have been developed, many of which are available for purchase. Examples of BPT programs include Russell Barkley's *Defiant Children* publication (Barkley, 2013), Alan Kazdin's *Parent Management Training* (Kazdin, 2005*), the Community Parenting Education Program* (COPE; Cunningham, Bremner, & Secord-Gilbert, 1998), and *Parent-Child Interaction Therapy* (PCIT; McNeil & Henbree-Kigin, 2010).

Chacko et al. (2015) outline common key components that typically comprise most BPT programs. Topics covered by most BPT programs are outlined in the following table.

Topics Covered in Most Behavioral Parent Training Interventions

Session Topic	Details
1. Psychoeducation	Information about ADHD, prognosis, treatments; ABC model in understanding behavior; reviewing the specific content of BPT sessions; conveying the importance of implementing all taught skills in a systematic and thoughtful manner.
2. Praise, Positive Attending, and Positive Parent-Child Quality Time	Praise when desired behavior is displayed; Positive Attending (e.g., eye contact; listening attentively; reflecting upon the child's verbal and nonverbal behavior); teach praising the "positive opposites" of negative behaviors—teach attending to desired behaviors rather than providing negative attention for problem behaviors; practice praise and positive attending within the context of identified child-centered quality times when the child is behaving appropriately.
3. Planned Ignoring	Ignore mildly annoying attention-seeking behaviors; teach parental emotion management and relaxation techniques to use during ignoring; emphasize importance of consistency in ignoring such behavior.
4. Effective Commands	1. Parents may give commands only when they have the ability to follow through with consequences for non-compliance. 2. Use commands conservatively. Determine if a command is necessary to achieve the desired outcome. 3. Give commands in a statement, not question, form. 4. Obtain the child's attention prior to giving a command.

	5. Commands need to be simple, clear, and comprise a single step. 6. Use transitional warnings as appropriate. 7. How to use "when–then" commands. 8. Allow the child to process and to comply with the request. If the child is noncompliant, restate the command accompanied by the consequences of ongoing noncompliance. 9. Praise compliance or implement consequence for repeated noncompliance immediately after the behavior occurs.
5. Incentive Systems	Reward systems, token economies; developing a structured system where the child may earn tangible reinforcement (e.g., rewards, privileges) contingent upon the display of specifically defined behavior.
6. Time-Out from Positive Reinforcement	A consequence-focused strategy; use after praise, positive attending, planned ignoring, and incentive systems are not successful; possibly implement when the child engages in attention-seeking behavior, when the child's goal is to obtain a tangible item, or when he or she is too emotionally dysregulated to engage in productive verbal communication; discuss with parents past experiences with time-out, logistics; troubleshoot as needed.
7. Problem solving	Teaching a structured format to implement when faced with specific problems. Structured problem-solving interventions generally involve teaching the following steps: 1. Identify the problem. 2. Define the problem concisely. 3. Brainstorm all potential solutions. 4. Evaluate potential advantages and disadvantages of each potential solution. 5. Eliminate the identified solution(s) with low likelihood of advantages. 6. Consider possibly combining remaining solutions in order to obtain a more effective solution. 7. Decide on a solution. Implement the solution. 8. Evaluate the outcome.

Behavioral/Family Interventions for Adolescents with ADHD

Behavioral Parent Training has been demonstrated to be most effective in preschool and school-age children. Aspects of BPT can also be applied with parents who have adolescents who demonstrate ADHD. However, the skills taught in these structured programs alone usually do not suffice. Interventions for such adolescents typically need to also focus on supporting communication between these youth and their parents. This includes mutually agreed-upon expectations of behavior and consequences. One excellent structured treatment intervention program following such a model is the *Defiant Teens* program developed by Russell Barkley and Arthur Robin (Barkley & Robin, 2014).

Arthur Robin (2015) presents a slightly modified variant of a structured behavioral intervention program to employ with parents and youth as compared to the approach outlined in the *Defiant Teens* manual (Barkley & Robin, 2014). Dr. Robin outlines a step-by-step approach of topics and techniques to be covered at each session. Illustrative examples are provided. Most clinicians could probably implement this program with their patients given the detailed information that is presented in this chapter. This intervention program is appropriate for adolescents ages 12 to 18 years who display ADHD with an externalizing behavioral disorder (e.g., Oppositional Defiant Disorder, Conduct Disorder). Both the adolescent and parent are involved in sessions. Most of the steps included in this treatment approach mirror those from the *Defiant Teens* manual albeit Robin notes a few specific differences. The steps of this intervention approach are outlined in the following table.

Steps	Details
#1 Education involving parents and the teen	(1) The first part of the session involves providing parents education regarding: a) ADHD, b) coercive exchanges, c) the four-factor model, d) the problem-solving communication model. (2) The second half of the session involves the youth alone. Education is provided regarding ADHD and treatment options; the therapist listens to the teen's reaction to this education; the therapist uses cognitive restructuring to address any expressed ADHD myths and to promote a positive attitude toward treatment.
#2 Education involving parents alone	Teaching parents 20 specific principles to consider in parenting an adolescent with ADHD.
#3 Fostering realistic beliefs and expectations	This step usually involves two full sessions. One is with parents alone while the other is with the adolescent alone. Parents are offered information regarding adolescent development to assist in helping them develop realistic expectations of behavior. Cognitive restructuring is used to help parents develop reasonable beliefs about their child's behavior. Emphasis is placed on understanding negative

	behaviors that all adolescents generally demonstrate. The session with the adolescent also involves cognitive restructuring addressing any unrealistic expectations and beliefs he or she may have.
#4 Preparing families for medication	This session involves meeting with parents and the child separately. Education is provided regarding medication for ADHD and the willingness of parents and the youth to pursue medication management, and a referral is provided to an appropriate physician as needed.
#5 Breaking the negativity cycle: One-on-one time	This step involves teaching parents to engage with their child in a positive manner. Parents are asked to spend 15 to 20 minutes of one-to-one time with their child five times per week in an enjoyable activity chosen by the child. Parents are taught to be accepting during the activity, which includes making only neutral or positive comments. The idea is for the child to experience their parent as nondemanding, noncritical, attentive, and positive. Any difficulties that may arise are problem-solved in-session. Progressing to Step #6 does not occur until this step has been fully implemented.
#6 Praise, Ignoring, Commands	Parents are taught how to praise positive behaviors, how to ignore minor negative behaviors, and how to give effective commands.
#7 Implementing Positive Incentive Systems	This step involves developing a behavioral contract where the adolescent may earn rewards and/or privileges contingent upon the display of specific target behaviors.
#8 Implementing Punishment Systems	Parents are taught how and when to implement specific punishment techniques (e.g., removal of privileges, response cost, grounding, work detail).
#9 Problem-solving negotiable issues	Parents and adolescents attend this session together. They are taught a structured problem-solving method to assist in resolving negotiable problems and to improve their communication.
#10 Improving Communication	This step often involves two to three sessions. Adolescents and parents attend these sessions together. A structured method is employed to help families identify their negative communication habits. Participants are then taught a range of more positive communication strategies to employ in situations where one is attempting to communicate disagreement, negative affect, or pointing out that the other person's behavior is not acceptable. Role playing is conducted. The therapist provides feedback as needed. The therapist also points out any specific negative communication patterns that are observed, intervenes, and provides corrective feedback as needed.

(Continued)

Steps	Details
#11 Putting it all together	Step 11 is jointly attended by parents and the child. This step usually requires one or two sessions and generally involves a review of previously taught principles and techniques from prior steps. Feedback is given as needed to modify any strategies and to improve their actual use. Referrals are made to other professionals (e.g., for marital therapy, psychiatric management addressing comorbid psychiatric disorders displayed by the parent or adolescent) as needed.

Other Treatment Implications for Adolescents with ADHD

Some other issues may need to be addressed when working with adolescents who demonstrate ADHD. The prefrontal cortex of the adolescent brain is a work in progress. The frontal lobes are not fully developed until one's early to mid-20s. ADHD is a neurobiological condition that primarily impacts frontal lobe functioning. Adolescents with ADHD may demonstrate particular challenges with problem solving, judgment, insight, impulsivity, and regulating other aspects of their emotions and behavior. This may manifest in a range of risk-taking behaviors related to driving, cell phone usage, social media/Internet interactions, substance use, medication misuse, and diversion of stimulant medication.

Adolescents with ADHD and their parents should be provided education regarding these issues. Parents should monitor for potential substance use. Urine drug-screening kits are available from most pharmacies at a low price. Random drug screens may be considered if there are concerns regarding substance usage.

Clinicians should consider discussing the proper use of stimulant medication with adolescents and their parents. Overuse and misuse can potentially lead to negative outcomes. All parties need to recognize that stimulant medications are considered controlled substances. Diverting such medication to others can potentially lead to serious legal consequences. Many physicians may also be reluctant to continue prescribing such medication if there is evidence of overuse, misuse, or diversion.

Behavioral contracting should be considered in relation to driving, cell phone use, and Internet privileges. Such contracting generally involves the youth agreeing to demonstrate specific responsible behaviors in order to continue accessing such privileges. It is ideal to establish such behavioral contracts within the therapeutic sessions.

Behavior modification for children with ADHD primarily involves the implementation of such strategies by the adults in the child's life (e.g., parents, teachers). Older children and adolescents can often benefit from learning how to independently implement a range of such behavioral strategies in order to improve their functioning. These techniques may include strategies for self-monitoring of their behavior, scheduling, organization, time management, academic skills building (e.g., specific study and test-taking strategies), and so forth.

Older adolescents need to be versed in a range of ADHD-related issues to help them prepare for the transition to adulthood. This includes ensuring they are aware of their ADHD history and other pertinent history (e.g., if they display a comorbid learning disorder or psychiatric condition) and that they possess the skills to effectively self-manage their ADHD-medication (e.g., independently making appointments with their physician, psychologist, or therapist; obtaining prescribed medication from the pharmacy; taking medication independently as prescribed).

Parents and the teen may need to discuss any ongoing parental support that may be needed in the child's early adult years. This may include monitoring or assistance with money management, paying bills, and the child's capacity to live independently. Such young adults may also need to be educated regarding how to access academic support services and accommodations at the college level. They may need similar education in regard to accessing reasonable accommodations in the workplace.

Classroom Management Strategies

ADHD is a neurodevelopmental condition that can affect the child's academic functioning. ADHD can have a negative impact on various aspects of learning and the child's academic grades. Many children with ADHD also struggle to control their behavior and emotions. This can potentially result in a range of disruptive behaviors demonstrated in the classroom and on the playground. Such impulsivity and disruptive behavior can also negatively impact the child's friendships and other social interactions.

A number of studies have examined the efficacy of various classroom interventions on ADHD-related symptomatology, disruptive behavior, and on-task behavior. Effective techniques are presented in the following table.

Classroom Intervention Strategies for Children with ADHD

Intervention	Description
Antecedent-based	This intervention involves manipulating antecedent conditions. This may involve changes in the environment, task, or instruction. Examples include: a) seating the child in the front of the classroom, near the teacher, and away from distractions; b) computer-assisted instruction; c) tutoring; d) choice making.
Consequence-based	This intervention employs reinforcement and punishment to change the frequency of the identified target behavior. Examples include: a) praise; b) rewards; c) access to privileges; d) response cost; e) verbal corrections.
Self-regulation	The child is taught self-control and problem-solving skills to regulate their thoughts and behavior. Examples include: a) self-reinforcement; b) self-monitoring; c) self-instruction.

Gaastra, Groen, Tucha, and Tucha (2016) performed a meta-analysis in regard to the effectiveness of the aforementioned classroom interventions in decreasing off-task and disruptive classroom behavior in children with ADHD. Both within-subjects design (WSD) and single-subject design (SSD) were employed and each study was analyzed separately. The researchers' analyses of WSD studies showed significant effects for all three types of interventions. Results indicated that consequence-based interventions had the most robust effect size ($M_{SMD} = 1.82$), and were more effective in reducing disruptive and off-task behaviors as compared to antecedent-based ($M_{SMD} = 0.31$), self-regulation ($M_{SMD} = 0.56$), and combined ($M_{SMD} = 0.58$) interventions. In contrast, SSD studies demonstrated largest effects for self-regulation interventions ($M_{SMD} = 3.61$), and smallest effects for consequence-based interventions ($M_{SMD} = 2.47$). The authors pose that these discrepant results between WSD and SSD studies may be a function of differences between subject characteristics (e.g., medication use) or the specific interventions that were implemented. They conclude that all of these interventions demonstrated positive effects on off-task and disruptive behavior. The effects of the specific intervention differed, ranging from small to large, and consequence-based and self-regulation interventions demonstrated the largest effects.

Pfiffner and DuPaul (2015) outline a range of classroom-based strategies that have been demonstrated to be effective with children who demonstrate ADHD. They also outline in this review a number of other issues to consider in the school setting. Key principles and techniques are as follows:

1. Educate teachers regarding ADHD. Educate teachers that children with ADHD need more structure, frequent positive consequences, consistent negative consequences, and accommodations to classroom expectations and assigned work.
2. Use interventions that manipulate antecedent events (e.g., preferential seating, modifying instruction).
3. Use positive reinforcement (e.g., praise) following the demonstration of a target behavior.
4. Use peers, parents, computer technology, or the child themselves to deliver classroom interventions.
5. Focus on teaching the child a set of skills and adaptive behaviors to replace the problem behaviors.
6. Reinforce academic performance (e.g., amount of work completed accurately) rather than just on-task behavior.
7. Target behaviors during transitions between classes/activities, recess, and lunch.
8. Ensure that the classroom is well-organized, structured, and predictable. Post a daily schedule, classroom rules, and other visual aids.
9. Teach classroom rules and expectations to all students.
10. Alter academic assignments to enhance the performance of the child who displays ADHD. For example: vary the format/materials to help maintain interest and motivation; make academic assignments brief; schedule as many academic subjects as possible in the morning hours; implement accommodations (e.g., extra time, reduced length of assignment/test; provide choices).

11. Use computer-assisted instruction.
12. Use explicit-instruction teaching techniques.
13. Provide instruction in regard to time management, organization, note-taking strategies, and so forth.
14. Introduce peer tutoring.
15. Use positive (e.g., praise, rewards, token economy) and negative (e.g., reprimands, time-out, response cost) consequences. Consequences must be immediate, brief, consistent, salient, and for positive consequences frequent.
16. Use Daily Report Cards targeting classroom participation, academic work, completion of homework, interactions, and behavior.
17. Teach self-regulation strategies (e.g., self-monitoring, self-reinforcement, self-instruction, problem solving).
18. Communicate and work with parents to promote maintenance and generalization of skills outside of the school setting.

It is usually important that the student with ADHD is identified for services through the Individuals with Disabilities Education Act (IDEA) and that a 504 Plan (or equivalent thereof in a private school) is established. This is important so that the child can qualify for services. Accommodations and other assistance for ADHD will often not be offered to the child by most school districts until it is determined that the child meets criteria for Section 504 of the IDEA.

Neurofeedback

Neurofeedback is an intervention that has been proposed as being efficacious for children and adolescents who demonstrate ADHD. The premise of neurofeedback is that the procedure targets dysfunctional patterns of brain activity that are believed to underlie ADHD. It is believed that symptoms of ADHD can be reduced through such treatment. This is accomplished via training the child in self-regulation techniques using operant reinforcement. Cortical activity derived from select electroencephalogram (EEG) data is converted into audio and/or visual signals that are fed back to the patient in real time. This data is typically presented on a computer screen. It may be represented by the speed or height of a balloon, ball, car, or other such animation. Learning of self-regulation is apparent when the child makes the object on the screen rise, fall, or move quicker.

A meta-analysis performed by Sonuga-Barke, Brandeis, Cortese and et al. (2013) examined the efficacy of neurofeedback on ADHD symptoms. This analysis included randomized treatment outcome trials only (n = 8). This meta-analysis also included an examination of outcomes rated by persons to be the most proximal to the therapeutic setting (i.e., usually parents who were not blinded) and ratings provided by reporters determined to be probably blinded. Results indicated that the impact of neurofeedback on ADHD total symptoms based on most proximal ratings were significant (Mean$_{SMD}$ = 0.59); this result generally reflects a moderate effect size. However, when only blinded outcome measures were examined the effects of neurofeedback were not significant (Mean$_{SMD}$ = 0.29).

A recent meta-analysis examining the efficacy of neurofeedback for ADHD was conducted by Cortese and colleagues (2016). These authors included 13 well-controlled treatment outcome trials (520 subjects, ages 3 to 18 years) in this analysis. Results reflected significant effects of neurofeedback on ADHD symptoms as rated by unblinded raters. Small significant effect sizes were noted for: ADHD total symptoms (Mean$_{SMD}$ = 0.35), inattention (Mean$_{SMD}$ = 0.36), and hyperactivity/impulsivity (Mean$_{SMD}$ = 0.26). Outcome data generated by blinded raters revealed nonsignificant effects for all measures: ADHD total symptoms (Mean$_{SMD}$ = 0.15), inattention (Mean$_{SMD}$ = 0.06), and hyperactivity/impulsivity (Mean$_{SMD}$ = 0.15). Pooling of results generated by objective neuropsychological instruments also revealed nonsignificant effects in relation to measures of attention (Mean$_{SMD}$ = 0.13) and inhibition (Mean$_{SMD}$ = 0.30).

Neurofeedback remains an intriguing nonpharmacological intervention that may at some point potentially be an efficacious treatment for children who demonstrate ADHD. This procedure warrants further research in relation to the development of other neurofeedback methods, electrode placements, standardization of neurofeedback protocols, and perhaps identifying specific predictors that relate to positive treatment outcomes. However, the current state of the literature does not appear to support neurofeedback as an effective treatment for ADHD.

Other Interventions for ADHD

A number of alternative medicine and other interventions have been proposed for ADHD. These include yoga, tai chi, massage therapy, craniosacral therapy, meditation, homeopathy, applied kinesiology, chiropractic, acupuncture, occupational therapy (i.e., sensory integrational training, interactive metronome), caffeine, vision therapy, and anthroposophical therapy. The quality of study designs examining the efficacy of these interventions is generally poor. The number of studies is limited. The large majority fail to employ randomization. Most do not include adequate placebo, sham, or alternative treatments. Most do not employ blinded assessments. The available data does not support the effectiveness of any of these interventions in addressing any of the challenges faced by children and adolescents who display ADHD. The interested reader is referred to Bader and Adesman (2015) for a comprehensive review of complementary and alternative medicine interventions for ADHD.

CHAPTER 5

Case Studies

Psychological Evaluation
Confidential—For Professional Use Only

Name: Sylvia Middleton
DOB: XXXX
D(s)OE: XXX
Age: 11-7
Education: 6.5

Tests Administered and Procedures: Clinical Interviews (Sylvia, Mother); Review of Records; Mental Status Examination/Behavior Observations; Child Behavior Checklist (CBCL)—Parent Report; Youth Self-Report Form/Child Behavior Checklist (YSR/CBCL); Vanderbilt Teacher Behavior Evaluation Scale—Teacher Reports.

Reason for Referral and Identifying Information: Sylvia Middleton is 11 years and 7 months old. She is African American and is right-handed. She is referred for psychological assessment by Ted Mulvaney, MD, to rule out a possible Attention-Deficit/Hyperactivity Disorder (ADHD). Sylvia presents with complaints of inattention and poor academic achievement.

Relevant Background Information: Sylvia has reportedly received very poor grades this academic year. These academic struggles appear to have prompted the current exam. Sylvia is in grade six. Sylvia and her mother indicated that she has historically done well academically until this academic year. She has never experienced any difficulties with reading, spelling, written expression, or mathematics. She has been receiving As/Bs until this academic year. Both stated that her grades have significantly decreased this year to Bs and Cs.

Sylvia feels that she has trouble focusing. She said that such attentional difficulties are long standing but have especially been problematic this academic year. She said that she is easily distracted in class, forgets instructions and directions offered by teachers, and is poorly organized, and claims that she has often forgotten to turn in assignments and homework.

Sylvia's mother commented that teachers have raised concerns regarding inattention since perhaps the third grade. No evaluations were ever pursued given that Sylvia always seemed to do well academically prior to middle school. Her mother commented that she is very forgetful, often loses things, is easily distractible, does not follow through on tasks, fails to finish tasks, and often procrastinates. She noted that Sylvia tends to give up easily if she finds the tasks to be difficult. She added that Sylvia frequently daydreams and needs constant reminders. She said that she often has to repeat things to Sylvia given that she does not seem to be listening. Other family members have reportedly offered similar feedback regarding such inattention. All of these symptoms have been persistent since early childhood.

Sylvia and her mother were interviewed via a semistructured clinical interview to further understand other aspects of her psychological functioning. She has never displayed any significant behavioral problems. There is no indication of any trauma history. No psychosocial difficulties were expressed. Both Sylvia and her mother denied psychological symptoms consistent with any competing DSM-5 psychological disorders, including those pertaining to depression and anxiety.

Developmental History: Sylvia was born approximately four weeks early following an uncomplicated pregnancy. Her mother denied the use of alcohol, drugs, or tobacco during pregnancy. She weighed 4 lb. 10 oz. at birth. No birth trauma was reported. All developmental milestones were met on time.

Relevant Medical History: Positive for allergies. No other significant medical illnesses, injuries, or surgeries were reported. Vision and hearing are normal per recent exams.

Medications: Zyrtec 10 mg OTC/PRN. She is not prescribed any medication. She has never been prescribed psychotropic medication during her lifetime.

Psychiatric History: None reported.

Family History: A paternal uncle and three paternal cousins reportedly demonstrate ADHD. Sylvia's father reportedly acknowledges lifetime symptoms of inattention yet he has never pursued any sort of exam or treatment for this issue. Her mother has a history of some depression. Sylvia's two older brothers were diagnosed with ADHD at a young age.

Educational History: Sylvia is a sixth-grade student who is served in a mainstream classroom at Richard Per Middle School. She has never been academically retained, nor has she ever accessed special education services. No 504 Plan or IEP have been developed.

Inspection of her report cards from the fourth and fifth grades consistently revealed grades of As and Bs across subject areas. Her grades have significantly decreased this academic year. Her academic subjects revealed two Bs, three Cs, and a D (in math). These academic records also appear to indicate that she has not handed in multiple homework assignments.

Relevant Social History: Sylvia was born in Miami, Florida. She has been living in the Charleston, South Carolina area with her family since the age of six. She lives with her parents and two brothers aged 14 and 17 years. Sylvia reportedly has a good group of friends. She is active in her church's youth group and plays on her school's volleyball and basketball teams. No obvious familial or psychosocial difficulties were reported.

Test Results

Test scores are estimates of the attribute measured by the test. Used properly, test scores are combined with other relevant information to assist with decisions about an individual's level of functioning and needs.

When test scores are placed on common scale, or standardized, direct comparisons can be made among them.

1. **For Standard Scores (SS)** the average is 100, with 90 to 110 often considered the average range.
2. **For Scaled Scores (ScS)** the average is 10 and the average range is often from 8 to 12.

The Percentile is based on the Standard and Scaled Scores and provides an estimate of the percentage of persons in your/your child's age range or grade in school that, if tested, would earn lower scores. The average Percentile is 50 and the average range is usually considered to be between the 25th and 75th percentile.

Ranges of Standard and Scaled Scores in this report are described using various sets of terms chosen by the author or publisher of each test. The following is an example of one such system of descriptors:

Scaled Score	Standard Score	Percentile	Descriptor
17 to 20	131 and above	98 and above	Very Superior
15 to 16	121 to 130	92 to 98	Superior
13 to 14	111 to 120	77 to 91	High Average
8 to 12	90 to 110	25 to 75	Average
6 to 7	80 to 89	9 to 23	Low Average
4 to 5	70 to 79	2 to 8	Borderline
1 to 3	69 and below	2 and below	Extremely Low/ Impaired

T-scores, with an average of 50 and a typical average range of 40 to 60, make up another type of standardized score. T-scores are most often used with psychological and behavior rating scales. The behaviors most often measured by T-scores are either "adaptive" (e.g., Social Skills), where high scores are desirable and low scores suggest need for improvement, or "clinical," where high scores may indicate a problem needing to be addressed and lower scores are considered normal or desirable. Scores from many tests examining different cognitive abilities (e.g., memory, attention, language) are often expressed in T-scores. Higher scores typically mean better functioning (e.g., above-average language skills) while lower scores typically mean poorer functioning (e.g., deficits of memory/ attention). Since Percentiles are not always based directly on T-scores, they are not included in the following table. This table shows a sample system of descriptors that might be used for adaptive, clinical, and neuropsychological test scores:

Adaptive Scales:		Clinical Scales:	
T-score range	Descriptor	T-score range	Descriptor
70 and above	Very High	70 and above	Clinically Significant
60 to 69	High	60 to 69	At-Risk
41 to 59	Average	41 to 59	Average

| 31 to 40 | At-Risk | 31 to 40 | Low |
| 30 and below | Clinically Significant | 30 and below | Very Low |

| Neuropsychological/Cognitive Scales: | |
T-score range	Descriptor
70 and above	Very Superior
63 to 69	Superior
57 to 62	High Average
44 to 56	Average
37 to 43	Low Average
31 to 36	Borderline
< 31	Deficient

Mental Status Examination/Behavioral Observations: Sylvia presented to the clinic with her mother. She appeared her stated age. She was in no obvious distress. Sylvia was alert and oriented to person, place, time, and situation. Grooming and appearance were neat and appropriate. Eye contact was good. Spontaneous speech was fluent, of normal pace and prosody, and without indication of any obvious expressive language delays. Receptive language appeared grossly intact. Thoughts were concrete to abstract, age appropriate, logical, and organized. Attention and concentration were somewhat weak. She did not evidence signs of hyperactivity or impulsivity. Mood was euthymic. Affect was congruent and appropriate. Her social skills were good. Sylvia's insight and judgment appeared good for her age. She denied suicidal ideation, plan, or intent. She was cooperative and respectful throughout this exam. Results are deemed reliable and valid.

Structured Clinical Interview for ADHD: Sylvia and her mother were independently interviewed via a structured clinical interview (i.e., Barkley & Murphy, 2006) to objectively assess symptoms associated with an Attention-Deficit/Hyperactivity Disorder. Symptoms of inattention have reportedly been persistent since the age of 8 years. Examples were offered illustrating how these symptoms have negatively impacted Sylvia at home, in sports, in her interactions with others, in academic performance, and in managing other daily responsibilities. Six or more symptoms of inattention and/or six or more symptoms of hyperactivity/ impulsivity may suggest the presence of an Attention-Deficit/Hyperactivity Disorder. Results were as follows:

Informant	# Attention Symptoms	Significant?	# Hyperactivity/ Impulsivity Symptoms	Significant?
Mother	9	Yes	1	No
Sylvia	6	Yes	2	No

Psychological/Behavioral Functioning: The *CBCL* provides a measure of children's and adolescents' behavior, psychological functioning, and competencies as viewed by parents and other caregivers. Sylvia's mother completed this measure. The *YSR/CBCL* provides a measure of children's and adolescents' behavior, psychological functioning, and competencies as viewed by themselves. Sylvia completed this measure. T-scores > 69 are clinically significant. T-scores of 65 to 69 are considered borderline clinically significant. Ratings resulted in the following scores.

Child Behavior Checklist (Ratings by Sylvia and Her Mother)

Syndrome Scales	Mother's Ratings (T-Scores)	Sylvia's Ratings (T-Scores)
Anxious/Depressed	53	50
Withdrawn/Depressed	52	50
Somatic Complaints	53	53
Social Problems	50	50
Thought Problems	52	50
Attention Problems	78*	70**
Rule-Breaking Behavior	54	55
Aggressive Behavior	51	50

* significant ** borderline significant

DSM-Oriented Scales	Mother's Ratings (T-Scores)	Sylvia's Ratings (T-Scores)
Affective Problems	52	54
Anxiety Problems	53	52

Somatic Problems	52	52
Attention-Deficit/ Hyperactivity Problems	70*	66**
Oppositional Defiant Problems	54	52
Conduct Problems	50	50

* significant ** borderline significant

Both Sylvia and her mother noted adequate competence across domains. Both endorsed symptoms reflecting significant attentional difficulties. Neither endorsed significant symptoms reflecting any behavioral disturbances, social difficulties, depression, anxiety, or other psychological concerns.

Two teachers independently completed the *Vanderbilt Teacher Behavior Evaluation Scale* to gain measures of behavior within the classroom setting. Both teachers endorsed significant symptoms of–inattention. Neither endorsed significant symptoms of hyperactivity or impulsivity. Neither teacher raised concerns regarding disruptive behavior, academic delays, or any psychological concerns. Results are presented in the following table.

Vanderbilt Teacher Behavior Evaluation Scale

Informant	# Attention Symptoms	Significant?	# Hyperactivity/ Impulsivity Symptoms	Significant?
Mrs. B	9	Yes	1	No
Mr. A	8	Yes	1	No

Diagnostic Impression (DSM-5)

1. Attention-Deficit/Hyperactivity Disorder Predominantly Inattentive Presentation

Discussion: Developmental history, structured clinical interviews, behavior observations, and psychological/behavior checklists are consistent with a diagnosis (DSM-5) of an Attention-Deficit/Hyperactivity

Disorder Predominantly Inattentive Presentation. Psychological exam was not consistent with any competing DSM-5 psychological disorders.

Recommendations: The results of this evaluation were reviewed with Sylvia and her mother. Education was provided regarding these results, ADHD, and treatment options. The following recommendations are offered.

1. Medication management as prescribed, monitored, and recommended by Dr. Mulvaney. Sylvia appears to be a good candidate for stimulant medication targeting ADHD. Please discuss medication options with Dr. Mulvaney in light of the current test results.

2. Behavior modification strategies are also important in the management of ADHD. I counseled Sylvia and her mother in a range of potential behavior modification strategies to apply at home and for school. I also gave them handouts outlining some other behavior modification strategies to implement for school and home. I recommend that Sylvia and her parents review this information and discuss a plan to implement specific strategies.

3. Please bring a copy of this report to Sylvia's school. Specific accommodations and recommendations are of course deferred to the school district's multidisciplinary team. Please consider developing a 504 Plan for this student given functional academic difficulties stemming from ADHD. The following suggestions may be helpful.

    1. Provide preferential seating in the front of the classroom.

    2. Repeat directions on an individual basis as needed.

    3. Maintain eye contact with student during verbal directions.

    4. Check student for understanding.

    5. Provide extra test-taking time (1.5x) as needed.

    6. Allow this student to take exams in a reduced-distraction environment.

    7. Check to ensure that student wrote down the correct assignment/homework information.

    8. Check to ensure that student handed in the necessary assignment/homework.

    9. Develop a regular communication system (e.g., e-mail) with her parents.

I appreciate the kind referral and opportunity to participate in Sylvia's care. I will be available for additional consultation as necessary.

Gordon Teichner, PhD, ABPP
Licensed Clinical Psychologist, SC #800
Board Certified in Clinical Psychology, American Board of Professional Psychology

Psychological Evaluation
Confidential—For Professional Use Only

Name: Robin Milakovich
DOB: XXXX
D(s)OE: XXX
Age: 8-4
Education: 3.2

Tests Administered and Procedures: Clinical Interviews (Robin, Mother, Father); Review of Records; Mental Status Examination/Behavior Observations; Structured Clinical Interview for ADHD (Barkley & Murphy, 2006); Conners 3 (Short Form)—Parent Reports (Two); Conners 3 (Short Form)—Teacher Reports (Two)

Reason for Referral and Identifying Information: Robin Milakovich is 8 years and 4 months old. He is Caucasian. He is referred for psychological assessment by his psychiatrist Stephen Choi, MD. Evaluation was requested to assist in diagnostic clarification and to aid in treatment planning. Robin presents with complaints of possible inattention, overactivity, and disruptive behavior.

Relevant Background Information: Robin's parents raised concerns regarding possible ADHD. Per a structured clinical interview, both independently endorsed all symptoms comprising the ADHD symptom clusters of Hyperactivity and Impulsivity. Both also endorsed most symptoms comprising the ADHD symptom cluster of Inattention. Teachers have also reportedly raised concerns regarding these symptoms and behaviors. Symptoms are demonstrated across settings and have been persistent since a very young age. Examples were offered illustrating how these symptoms have negatively impacted Robin's functioning across a range of his life's activities.

Robin's parents also raised concerns regarding very disruptive behavior. His parents are divorced. Such disruptive behavior has been displayed at both homes. Similar behavior has reportedly been demonstrated with both sets of grandparents. Multiple complaints from school have been offered regarding the same type of behavioral disturbances since preschool.

Robin reportedly demonstrates frequent temper tantrums. Such tantrums are almost always precipitated by situations where he does not get his way, when the answer is no, or when a request is made in regard to something that he does not want to do. He reportedly is extremely argumentative, defiant, and easily frustrated. Robin often appears angry and resentful. Rarely does he take responsibility for his behavior. He usually blames others for his misbehavior. He often purposely annoys others. His parents added that he is often vindictive. Lying has also been problematic. Such behavior has been persistent since perhaps the age of four.

Robin's parents raised concerns regarding his social skills. They said that he has struggled to make and keep friends. He wants to have friendships and interact with other children. However, he has reportedly often alienated other children given his behavior. His parents said that he is very bossy and demanding, and it is essentially "… his way or the highway." Teachers have reported frequent conflict with peers at school.

Per semistructured clinical interviews, neither Robin nor either of his parents endorsed symptoms consistent with any mood disorders (e.g., a Depressive Disorder, Bipolar Disorder), anxiety disorders, or other DSM-5 psychological conditions. No lifetime trauma incidents were reported.

Available for my review were Parent and Teacher Vanderbilt Scales completed by Robin's mother and his second-grade teacher. These measures were completed approximately six months ago and were distributed by his pediatrician. Both measures yielded ratings that often relate to a diagnosis of ADHD Combined Presentation. Both instruments also reflected the endorsement of significant oppositional and other defiant behaviors. Robin's mother stated that his pediatrician offered an opinion that Robin probably demonstrates ADHD. His pediatrician recommended a medication trial but neither parent wished to put him on medication at that time.

Developmental History: Robin was born three weeks early following an uncomplicated pregnancy. His mother did not use alcohol, drugs, or tobacco products during this pregnancy. He weighed 6 lb. 7 oz. at birth. No birth traumas were reported. All developmental milestones were met on time.

Relevant Medical History: Positive for allergies and asthma, which are controlled. He is status post tonsillectomy. No other significant medical illnesses or injuries were reported. Recent hearing and vision exams were normal.

Medications: Singulair 10 mg QD; albuterol inhaler PRN. Robin has never been prescribed psychotropic medication during his lifetime.

Psychiatric History: Robin has seen Dr. Choi for an initial intake session. No other lifetime psychological or psychiatric contacts were reported.

Family History: Robin's father reported that he was diagnosed with ADHD during childhood and was prescribed Ritalin. Robin's two paternal uncles were diagnosed with ADHD during childhood as well. He has three male paternal first cousins, who are sons of these uncles, who also display this condition. Robin's mother stated that she has "anxiety." Robin's maternal grandmother has reportedly been diagnosed with Obsessive-Compulsive Disorder. Robin's mother stated that multiple maternal relatives have displayed a range of substance abuse problems.

Educational History: Robin is a third-grade student who attends the Francis Bautista Academic Academy. No academic delays were reported. His parents described him as an "Average" student (i.e., receiving Bs/Cs). Teachers have reportedly commented that he is a bright child who is not living up to his full academic potential. Robin has never been academically retained. No 504 Plan or IEP have been developed.

Inspection of Robin's report cards confirms the grades reported by his parents. These records also document that current and prior teachers have consistently raised concerns regarding inattention, impulsivity, disruptive behavior, and poor peer relations.

Relevant Social History: Robin was born in Vancouver, Canada. His family moved to the United States when he was an infant. His parents divorced when he was three years old. Both have remarried. Robin does not have any siblings. He primarily resides with his mother and stepfather in a home that is located in Summerville, South Carolina. He spends time with his father and stepmother every Wednesday evening and every other weekend. He reportedly likes both stepparents.

Robin is not currently involved in any extracurricular activities. He was previously involved in soccer and the Boy Scouts. However, neither activity worked out well. Robin reportedly initiated multiple conflicts with peers at both activities. As a result, the administrators asked his parents to withdraw him from these activities.

Robin's biological parents appear to be reasonably amicable and maintain good communication. No other obvious familial or psychosocial difficulties were reported.

Test Results

Mental Status Examination/Behavioral Observations: Robin came to my clinic with both parents. He presented as a large boy who seemed somewhat older than his stated age. He was alert and fully oriented. Eye contact was poor. His dress was casual and appropriate. Robin clearly demonstrated articulation difficulties in expressive speech. He struggled with "r" and "s" sounds; his parents commented that such articulation difficulties have been a lifelong problem. Otherwise, speech was generally fluent and of normal prosody and rate. Receptive language was grossly intact. Thoughts were concrete, age appropriate, and logical. There was no indication of an obvious thought disorder. Robin was extremely inattentive during this examination process. He required multiple prompts and redirection. He fidgeted constantly. He got out of his seat multiple times throughout the visit and touched various objects in my office. Both parents attempted to correct him on each occasion. He generally ignored both of their attempts at discipline. He did, however, comply when I asked him to stop and sit down. He was often loud, boisterous, and impulsive. He constantly interrupted me and both of his parents. He seemed completely unaware of how his behavior was inappropriate. Robin did not evidence any obvious sensory, perceptual, or motor deficits. He described his mood as "good." His parents commented that he is generally a happy child as long as things are going his way. Otherwise, he is prone to be irritable and will often throw a tantrum. His affect was generally euthymic and appropriate. Social skills were poor. Robin's insight and judgment appear poor. Results are deemed reliable and valid.

Structured Clinical Interview for ADHD: Robin's mother and father were independently interviewed via a structured clinical interview (i.e., Barkley & Murphy, 2006) to objectively assess symptoms associated with an Attention-Deficit/Hyperactivity Disorder. Symptoms have reportedly been persistent since perhaps the age of four. Multiple examples were offered illustrating how these symptoms have negatively impacted Robin with his immediate family, at school, with his social interactions, in recreational activities, and in managing other daily responsibilities. Six or more symptoms of inattention and/or six or more symptoms of hyperactivity/impulsivity may suggest the presence of an Attention-Deficit/Hyperactivity Disorder. Results were as follows.

Informant	# Attention Symptoms	Significant?	# Hyperactivity/ Impulsivity Symptoms	Significant?
Mother	8	Yes	9	Yes
Father	7	Yes	9	Yes

Psychological/Behavioral Functioning: The *Conners 3* is an instrument designed for parents and teachers to rate the behavior of children and youth ages 6 to 18 years. This instrument yields information that can be helpful in identifying ADHD, behavioral difficulties, and problems with peer relationships that the child may display. Both parents independently completed this measure. Both of Robin's teachers also independently completed this instrument. Inspection of the Validity Scales indicated that all profiles were valid. Results (T-scores) are presented in the following tables.

Conners 3 Short Form: Parent Reports (T-Scores)

Informant	Inattention	Hyper- activity/ Impulsivity	Learning Problems	Executive Functioning	Defiance/ Aggression	Peer Relations
Mother	74	85	52	72	85	78
Father	70	78	55	70	78	75

T-score of 70+ = Very Elevated; T-score 65–69 = Elevated; T-score 60–64 = High Average; T-score 40–59 = Average; T-score <40 = Low

Conners 3 Short Form: Teacher Reports (T-Scores)

Informant	Inattention	Hyper- activity/ Impulsivity	Learning Problems / Executive Functioning	Defiance/ Aggression	Peer Relations
Ms. B	79	81	61	75	81
Ms. A	74	80	62	81	75

T-scores of 70+ = Very Elevated; T-score 65–69 = Elevated; T-score 60–64 = High Average; T-score 40–59 = Average; T-score <40 = Low

All informants reported significant symptoms of inattention, hyperactivity, and impulsivity. Robin's parents further endorsed a range of other executive difficulties reflecting poor planning, organization, procrastination, and prioritizing. All informants reported very problematic aggressive and defiant behaviors. Both parents and teachers further indicated poor social skills and related difficulties with peer relationships. Neither his parents nor teachers endorsed items that are reflective of characteristics of students with any learning or academic delays.

Diagnostic Impression (DSM-5)

1. Attention-Deficit/Hyperactivity Disorder Combined Presentation
2. Oppositional Defiant Disorder
3. Speech Sound Disorder

Discussion: Developmental history, structured clinical interviews, behavior observations, and psychological/behavior checklists are consistent with a diagnosis (DSM-5) of an Attention-Deficit/Hyperactivity Disorder Combined Presentation. Robin's other disruptive behavior warrants mention of a diagnosis (DSM-5) of an Oppositional Defiant Disorder. Robin also displays articulation difficulties that are consistent with a DSM-5 diagnosis of a Speech Sound Disorder. Psychological exam was not consistent with any other DSM-5 psychological disorders.

Recommendations: The results of this evaluation were reviewed with Robin's parents. Education was provided regarding these results, ADHD, Oppositional Defiant Disorder, Speech Sound Disorder, and treatment options. The following recommendations are offered.

1. Medication management as prescribed, monitored, and recommended by Dr. Choi. Robin appears to be a good candidate for psychostimulant medication targeting ADHD. Please discuss medication options with Dr. Choi in light of the current test results.
2. Behavior modification strategies are important in the management of ADHD. Some examples were briefly discussed. A handout outlining some techniques was given to his parents. Additional information is available via www.chadd.org, www.adhdandyou.com, and my

website at www.psychologist.iwarp.com. I recommend that Robin's family review such information and jointly discuss a specific plan of implementing such strategies.

3. The following are some general behavior management techniques and principles for his family to consider.

Behavior Management Principles and Techniques

Principles

- It is paramount to establish a **United Parenting Front**. It is important for parents to discuss the specifics of how they plan to initiate strategies and plans. All positive reinforcement and consequences must be delivered in the same way by all caregivers.
- **Be consistent**. Deliver all reinforcers/consequences *every time* as appropriate.
- The most effective way to change behavior is through **Positive Reinforcement**.
- **Be positive**.
- **No Dialogues**. Do not lecture. Be direct. Be brief and to the point (e.g., "I need you to start your homework," "Stop," "There is no hitting in this house," "There is no arguing.").
- **Say What You Mean and Mean What You Say**.
- **Model Appropriate Behavior** (e.g., responsibility, dependability, working hard, following through, talking calmly, being reasonable, no emotional outbursts, no negative communication, no negative behaviors, taking responsibility for behavior, solving problems appropriately, good manners, respect for others, prosocial behavior, not being overcontrolling, eating healthy, exercising, etc.). Remember that you are raising adults. Children of all ages are actively watching and learning from YOU. They often model their parents' behavior. Adults sometimes need to take a look at their own behavior and make changes in order to help their children. You cannot expect your child to display a certain behavior if you do not do it yourself.
- **Deliver Consequences as Appropriate**.

Techniques

- Paying attention to any behavior generally maintains or increases the behavior. Therefore, remember to:
  (1) Give *frequent* praise, attention, rewards, and so on for all appropriate and positive behaviors. "Catch" your child being good. Point out all the good things that your child is doing. Lay it on thick.
  (2) Ignore all minor annoying behaviors and transgressions.
- **Positive Communication**. Establish a list of "Communication Rules" (e.g., No: screaming, yelling, raising your voice, name calling, bringing up the past, blaming, making excuses, tantrums, nasty comments, etc.) that *all* (i.e., adults and children) family members agree to follow. Post this list on the fridge.
- Offer rewards or privileges for good behavior.
- Offer choices.
- Be consistent.
- Increase structured/fun activities.
- Increase compliments.
- Keep the rules simple.
- Provide structure and routine.
- Provide immediate feedback and encouragement.
- Develop a "reward system." Your child can earn rewards/privileges if displaying specific behaviors (e.g., good grades, completing of chores, absence of disruptive behavior).
- Corrective statements (e.g., "No hitting!").
- State instructions clearly. State consequence of what will happen if your child does not comply (i.e., give a warning); praise if the child complies.
- Response cost; take away a privilege (e.g., watching TV).
- Time-out. This is more for younger children. Have your child apologize and practice what he or she should have done in that situation when time-out is over.
- Positive practice; have your child practice appropriate behavior several times.

- Broken record technique; repeat your instructions calmly and repeatedly like a broken record.
- Listen to your child.
- Spend time with your child. Be active in your child's life.
- Help your child to identify their feelings.
- Help your child solve their problems as appropriate.
- Support the other parent.
- Do not discuss certain adult issues (e.g., annoyances that you may have with the other parent) with your child. Many adult issues need to be discussed solely between adults.

4. Individual psychological therapy for children with ADHD/ODD is largely ineffective. Research indicates that treatment efforts need to primarily involve parents. This will be a key therapeutic process to pursue.

    I believe that Robin's parents need to jointly attend Behavioral Parent Training (BPT). Such treatment typically involves weekly one-hour sessions. Most BPT programs involve around 12 sessions. A referral was sent to Dr. Jim Woskosky at the request of Robin's parents to link them with such treatment services.

5. Please bring a copy of this report to his school. Specific accommodations and recommendations are of course deferred to the multidisciplinary team. Results may assist in developing a 504 Plan for Robin given functional academic difficulties stemming from ADHD.

    It would be helpful if the school psychologist could develop a behavioral intervention plan given Robin's behavioral challenges. I would be happy to provide input if requested. Additionally, I believe that the school psychologist will likely need to offer ongoing consultation to Robin's classroom teacher in regard to a range of positive behavior modification strategies to employ.

    I recommend that the school develop some sort of communication system (e.g., e-mail) with his family. Linkage with a social skills training group, if available, would be helpful.

The following classroom behavior modification strategies and accommodations may be helpful.

1. Provide preferential seating in the front of the classroom.
2. Repeat directions on an individual basis as needed.
3. Maintain eye contact with student during verbal directions.
4. Check student for understanding.
5. Provide extra test-taking time (1.5x) as needed.
6. Allow the student to take exams in a reduced-distraction environment.
7. Check to ensure that student wrote down the correct assignment/homework information.
8. Check to ensure that student handed in the necessary assignment/homework.
9. Develop a regular communication system (e.g., e-mail) with his parents.

6. I recommend linkage with a speech therapist. Robin could benefit from speech therapy targeting the Speech Sound Disorder that he demonstrates. A referral was sent to Carolina Speech Therapy Associates at the request of his parents.

I appreciate the kind referral and opportunity to participate in Robin's care. I will be available for additional consultation as necessary.

Gordon Teichner, PhD, ABPP
Licensed Clinical Psychologist, SC #800
Board Certified in Clinical Psychology, American Board of Professional Psychology

Psychological Evaluation

Confidential—For Professional Use Only

Name: Brent E. Mykyte
DOB: XXXX
D(s)OE: XXXX
Age: 9-1

Tests Administered and Procedures

Clinical Interviews (Brent, Father)
Review of Records
Mental Status Examination/Behavior Observations
Wechsler Intelligence Scale for Children, Fourth Edition (WISC-IV)
Wechsler Individual Achievement Test, Third Edition (WIAT-III)
Conners Continuous Performance Test, Second Edition (CPT-II)
Comprehensive Test of Phonological Processing (CTOPP)
Children's Paced Auditory Serial Addition Test (CHIPASAT)
Beery-Buktenica Developmental Test of Visual-Motor Integration, Sixth
Edition (VMI-VI)
Child Behavior Checklist (CBCL); Parent Report
Child & Adolescent Symptom Inventory, Fifth Edition; Parent Report
Teacher Report Form/Child Behavior Checklist (TRF/CBCL)
Beck Depression Inventory—Youth
Beck Anxiety Inventory—Youth
Beck Self-Concept Inventory—Youth

Reason for Referral and Identifying Information: Brent Mykyte is a Caucasian boy who is 9 years and 1 month old. He is referred for psychological assessment by his therapist Trevor Beauchamp, LPC. Examination was requested to rule out possible learning disabilities, to rule out ADHD, to clarify anxiety-related issues, and to seek recommendations for treatment. Brent presents with complaints of inattention, anxiety, and possible academic delays.

Relevant Background Information: Per a structured clinical interview, Brent and his father endorsed most symptoms comprising the

ADHD symptom cluster of Inattention. Symptoms of hyperactivity, impulsivity, and other disruptive behavior are largely absent. Symptoms have reportedly been displayed across settings since kindergarten age. Multiple examples were offered illustrating how these symptoms have negatively impacted Brent's functioning in school, with his grades, in social relations, at home with his family, and in managing other aspects of his day-to-day activities.

Brent worries persistently and excessively regarding multiple issues. His father commented that he has been a worrier since a very young age. Brent and his father indicated that he worries excessively about school, his academic performance, how he is perceived by others, friendships, safety issues, the future, and multiple day-to-day little things. Brent finds it very difficult to control such worry. Such worry is present more days than not. When worrying, he often finds it difficult to relax, becomes restless and irritable, experiences stomachaches, notes increased inattention, and finds it difficult to get to sleep.

Per a semistructured clinical interview, both Brent and his father denied psychological symptoms consistent with any competing anxiety disorders. Both denied any mood difficulties, including those pertaining to depression. There is no trauma history. Psychological symptoms consistent with any competing DSM-5 disorders were denied.

Developmental History: Brent was delivered full term. He weighed 6 lb. at birth. No pregnancy- or birth-related difficulties were reported. His mother did not use alcohol or drugs during pregnancy. However, Brent's father said that she regularly smoked cigarettes throughout this pregnancy. Brent achieved all developmental milestones on time.

Medical History: Positive for allergies (controlled). He experienced chronic ear infections during infancy. Three sets of PE tubes were placed. No other significant medical illnesses, injuries, or surgeries were reported.

Result of a recent hearing exam was reportedly normal. Brent just started wearing glasses given that he is slightly nearsighted.

Medications: Zyrtec 10 mg QD. No lifetime psychotropic medication trials were reported.

Psychiatric History: Brent has seen a therapist (Trevor Beauchamp) for an initial intake session only. No other lifetime psychiatric or psychological contacts were reported.

Family History: Brent's father reported that he demonstrates anxiety. Brent has a maternal aunt who also displays anxiety. Brent's older brother has been identified with ADHD. No other familial history of any developmental or psychological disorders was offered.

Educational History: Brent is a third-grade student who is served in a mainstream classroom. He has never been academically retained. No IEP or 504 Plan have been developed.

Brent's father said that Brent has always struggled with reading and mathematics. Teachers have reportedly raised concerns regarding possible reading and math delays since the first grade. There was discussion of retaining Brent in the first grade. Brent has continued to have such academic difficulties even though he has been pursuing tutoring targeting math and reading for the past six months. In contrast, Brent has always reportedly done well in the realms of spelling and written expression. Report cards were requested; however, none were ever submitted for review.

Relevant Social History: Brent's father is 31 years old. He is a high school graduate who is employed as a longshoreman. Brent's mother is 29 years old. She also is a high school graduate. She is employed as an administrative assistant at a physician's office. Brent has an 11-year-old brother. Brent was born in Atlanta, Georgia. He moved to the Charleston area with his family approximately two years ago. He resides with both parents and his brother in a home that is located in North Charleston, South Carolina.

Brent is involved in some extracurricular activities, including karate and baseball. No concerns regarding his social skills were raised. He reportedly interacts well with other children and adults. No obvious psychosocial stressors were described other than the noted academic difficulties.

Test Results

Test scores are estimates of the attribute measured by the test. Used properly, test scores are combined with other relevant information to assist with decisions about an individual's level of functioning and needs.

When test scores are placed on common scale, or standardized, direct comparisons can be made among them.

- **For Standard Scores (SS)** the average is 100, with 90 to 110 often considered the average range.
- **For Scaled Scores (ScS)** the average is 10 and the average range is often from 8 to 12.

The Percentile is based on the Standard and Scaled Scores and provides an estimate of the percentage of persons in your/your child's age range or grade in school that, if tested, would earn lower scores. The average Percentile is 50 and the average range is usually considered to be between the 25th and 75th percentile.

Ranges of Standard and Scaled Scores in this report are described using various sets of terms chosen by the author or publisher of each test. The following is an example of one such system of descriptors:

Scaled Score	Standard Score	Percentile	Descriptor
17 to 20	131 and above	98 and above	Very Superior
15 to 16	121 to 130	92 to 98	Superior
13 to 14	111 to 120	77 to 91	High Average
8 to 12	90 to 110	25 to 75	Average
6 to 7	80 to 89	9 to 23	Low Average
4 to 5	70 to 79	2 to 8	Borderline
1 to 3	69 and below	2 and below	Extremely Low/ Impaired

T-scores, with an average of 50 and a typical average range of 40 to 60, make up another type of standardized score. T-scores are most often used with psychological and behavior rating scales. The behaviors most often measured by T-scores are either "adaptive" (e.g., Social Skills), where high scores are desirable and low scores suggest need for improvement, or "clinical," where high scores may indicate a problem needing to be addressed and lower scores are considered normal or desirable. Scores from many tests examining different cognitive abilities (e.g., memory, attention, language) are often expressed in T-scores. Higher scores typically mean better functioning (e.g., above-average language skills) while lower scores typically mean poorer functioning (e.g., deficits of memory/ attention). Since Percentiles are not always based directly on T-scores, they are not included in the following table. This table shows a sample system of descriptors that might be used for adaptive, clinical, and neuropsychological test scores:

Adaptive Scales:		Clinical Scales:	
T-score range	Descriptor	T-score range	Descriptor
70 and above	Very High	70 and above	Clinically Significant
60 to 69	High	60 to 69	At-Risk
41 to 59	Average	41 to 59	Average
31 to 40	At-Risk	31 to 40	Low
30 and below	Clinically Significant	30 and below	Very Low

Neuropsychological/Cognitive Scales:	
T-score range	Descriptor
70 and above	Very Superior
63 to 69	Superior
57 to 62	High Average
44 to 56	Average
37 to 43	Low Average
31 to 36	Borderline
<31	Deficient

Mental Status Examination/Behavior Observations: Brent presented as a well-developed little boy who appeared his stated age. Grooming and appearance were neat and appropriate. Spontaneous speech was fluent, of normal pace and prosody, and without indication of any articulation or other expressive language delays. Receptive language appeared grossly intact. His thoughts were concrete, age appropriate, logical, and organized. There was no indication of an obvious thought disorder. Problematic inattention was displayed throughout this exam. No signs of obvious hyperactivity or impulsivity were displayed. Brent did not demonstrate any obvious sensory, perceptual, or motor deficits per exam. He described his mood as, "I worry a lot." His affect was slightly anxious. Social skills were good. He seemed to have reasonably good insight and judgment for his age. He denied suicidal ideation, plan, or intent. Brent was respectful, cooperative, and demonstrated good testing effort throughout this examination process. Results are deemed a reliable and valid indication of his true abilities.

Intellectual Functioning: Brent was administered the *WISC-IV* to objectively assess intellectual functioning. Results are reported in the following.

WISC-IV

Composite Scores Summary

Scale	Composite Score	Percentile Rank	95 percent Confidence Interval	Qualitative Description
Verbal Compre-hension (VCI)	110	75	103–116	High Average
Perceptual Reasoning (PRI)	110	75	102–117	High Average
Working Memory (WMI)	83	13	77–92	Low Average
Processing Speed (PSI)	80	9	73–91	Low Average
Full Scale (FSIQ)	99	47	94–104	Average

Academic Achievement: Brent was administered the *WIAT-III* to objectively assess reading, reading comprehension, written expression, language, academic skills, and math abilities. Age norms were used in the interpretation. Standard scores and percentile ranks are reported in the following.

WIAT-III

Subtest Score Summary

Subtest	Standard Score	Percentile Rank
Reading Comprehension	108	70
Math Problem Solving	106	66
Sentence Composition	100	50
Word Reading	105	63
Pseudoword Decoding	103	58
Numerical Operations	104	61
Oral Reading Fluency	102	55
Spelling	104	61

Cumulative Percentages

Word Reading Speed	The score is the same as or higher than the scores obtained by 50 percent of students in the normative sample; 50 percent of students in the normative sample scored higher than this score.
Pseudoword Decoding Speed	The score is the same as or higher than the scores obtained by 50 percent of students in the normative sample; 50 percent of students in the normative sample scored higher than this score.

Subtest Component Score Summary

Sentence Composition	Standard Score	Percentile Rank
Sentence Combining	100	50
Sentence Building	101	53

Composite Scores Summary

Composite	Standard Score	Percentile Rank
Total Reading	105	63
Basic Reading	102	55
Reading Comprehension and Fluency	104	61
Mathematics	105	63

Attention: Brent was administered the *CPT-II* to objectively assess visual sustained attention, reaction time, inattention, and the ability to inhibit impulsive responses. The CPT discriminant function indicated that the results better matched a clinical (i.e., ADHD), as compared to nonclinical (i.e., Normal), profile. The Confidence Index (92.35 percent) can be described as chances are 92.35 out of 100 that a significant attention problem exists. Vigilance (i.e., sustained attention) fell within the markedly atypical range (T-score = 85). Reaction time was slow (T-score = 73) reflecting deficits of visual processing speed. Brent made excessive errors of omission (T-score = 91) reflecting severe deficits of visual focused attention. He did not make excessive errors of commission (T-score = 51) reflecting the absence of problematic impulsivity on this test administration.

Working memory (i.e., basic focused attention, immediate memory) was within the Low Average range (WISC-IV; WMI, SS = 83, 13th percentile). Performances on tasks examining speed of information processing fell within similar range limits (WISC-IV; PSI, SS = 80, 9th percentile). Both Index scores are statistically (p < .05) discrepant from his level of intellect.

Brent was administered the *CHIPASAT*. This task assesses auditory focused attention (working memory), divided attention, and information processing speed. His overall score fell in the Impaired range (<1st percentile).

Visuoperceptual: Brent was administered the *VMI-VI* to assess visuomotor-integrational skills. He obtained a score corresponding to the 81st percentile (SS = 113). This score falls in the High Average range.

Language/Phonological Processing: General verbal abilities fell within the High Average range (WISC-IV, VCI = 110, 75th percentile). Results of a task assessing pseudoword decoding fell within Average range parameters (WIAT-III; Pseudoword Decoding; SS = 103, 58th percentile).

Brent was administered the *CTOPP* to examine phonological processing abilities. Such skills are paramount in reading, written expression, and aspects of expressive language. Age norms were used in the interpretation. Test results were as follows.

CTOPP

Composites	Percentile rank	Index score
Phonological Awareness	63	105
Phonological Memory	75	110
Rapid Naming	58	103

Brent's *Phonological Awareness Index* fell strongly within Average range (SS = 105, 63rd percentile). Inspection of individual subtests comprising this index indicates that he demonstrates Average range skills related to removing phonological segments from spoken words to form other words. He also displays Average range abilities to synthesize sounds to form words. These are important skills related to the reading process.

Brent's *Phonological Memory Index* was within the High Average range (SS = 110, 75th percentile). Tasks comprising this index reflect an individual's ability to encode information phonologically for temporary storage in working or short-term memory. This performance reflects High Average range abilities in decoding new lengthy words.

Brent's *Rapid Naming Index* was in the Average range (SS = 103, 58th percentile). These results indicate that he demonstrates Average range abilities related to retrieving phonological information from long-term or permanent memory and executing a sequence of operations quickly and repeatedly. Efficient retrieval of phonological information and the execution of sequences and operations are required when readers attempt to decode unfamiliar words.

Structured Clinical Interview for ADHD: Brent and his father were independently interviewed via a structured clinical interview (i.e., Barkley & Murphy, 2006) to objectively assess symptoms associated with an Attention-Deficit/Hyperactivity Disorder. In general, they offered a similar report of symptoms. Symptoms are noted across settings, are long standing (i.e., persistent since the age of five), and appear have to have caused functional impairments. Six or more symptoms of inattention and/or six or more symptoms of hyperactivity/impulsivity may suggest the presence of an Attention-Deficit/Hyperactivity Disorder. Results were as follows.

Informant	# Attention Symptoms	Significant?	# Hyperactivity/ Impulsivity Symptoms	Significant?
Brent	6	Yes	2	No
Father	9	Yes	1	No

Psychological/Behavioral Functioning

Achenbach Child Behavior Checklist (CBCL): The *Child Behavior Checklist (CBCL/6-18)* provides a measure of children's and adolescents' behavior, psychological functioning, and competencies as viewed by parents and other caregivers. Brent's father completed this instrument. The *Teacher Report Form (TRF/CBCL)* provides a measure of children's and adolescents' behavior, psychological functioning, and competencies as viewed by teachers and other school personnel. Brent's teacher completed this instrument. T-scores ≥ 70 are clinically significant. T-scores of 65 to 69 are considered borderline clinically significant. Results were as follows.

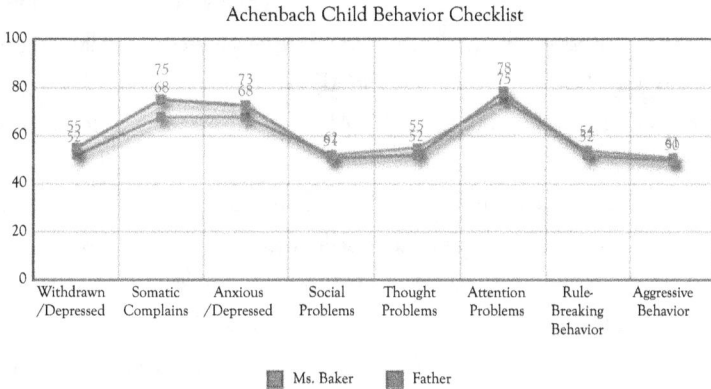

Achenbach Child Behavior Checklist

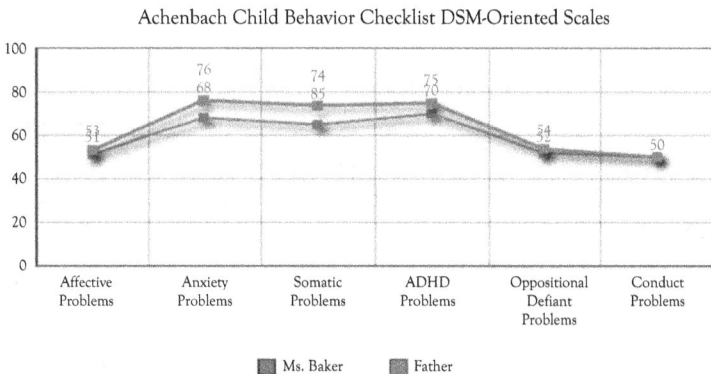

Achenbach Child Behavior Checklist DSM-Oriented Scales

The CBCL Competence Scale scores are not presented in the preceding figures. Per these scales, Brent's father and teacher raised concerns regarding his academic achievement. Competency across other domains (e.g., participation in activities, social functioning) fell strongly within Average range parameters. Brent's father and teacher endorsed items reflecting very problematic inattention. His father endorsed symptoms reflecting very problematic anxiety along with the observation of excessive somatic complaints. Brent's teacher noted borderline significant symptoms of anxiety and somatic complaints. Neither endorsed difficulties with aggression, defiance, conduct problems, or other disruptive behavior. Neither raised concerns regarding any interpersonal difficulties, depression, or other psychological issues.

Child & Adolescent Symptom Inventory—Fifth Edition (CASI-5): Brent's father completed the *CASI-5* Parent Report. This is an objective self-report of symptoms associated with many DSM-5 childhood behavioral and psychological disorders. Ratings yielded the following statistically significant scale elevations: ADHD Predominantly Inattentive Type; Generalized Anxiety Disorder. All other Clinical Scales fell strongly within normal range limits.

Beck Youth Inventories—Second Edition: The *Beck Youth Inventories-II* assesses children and adolescents ages 7 through 18 years for depression, anxiety, and self-concept. Brent completed these self-report measures. He reported an adequate self-concept. He did not endorse problematic symptoms of depression. Brent did, however, endorse very problematic symptoms of anxiety. Results are presented in the following table.

Scores: Beck Youth Inventories-II

Beck Youth Inventories-II	T-Score
Beck Anxiety Inventory—Youth	72***
Beck Depression Inventory—Youth	45
Beck Self-Concept Inventory—Youth	52

* mildly elevated range, ** moderately elevated range, ***severely elevated range

Diagnostic Impression (DSM-5/ICD-10)

1. Attention-Deficit/Hyperactivity Disorder Predominantly Inattentive Presentation
2. Generalized Anxiety Disorder
3. No indication of any Specific Learning Disorder

Discussion: Overall intellectual abilities fell strongly with in the Average range of functioning (FSIQ = 99). However, Brent's intellectual abilities are perhaps best understood via inspection of his WISC-IV verbal and nonverbal intellectual indixes. Both verbal (VCI = 110) and nonverbal (PRI = 110) intellectual abilities are well developed given scores falling in the High Average ranges. His verbal and nonverbal intellectual skills are equally developed. Inspection of WISC-IV subtests revealed significant weaknesses on tasks examining aspects of working memory and information processing speed.

Examination results reflected Average (i.e., normal) range abilities of phonological processing. Such skills are important in language, reading, and written expression. All results were generally commensurate with his level of intellect. Test results also reflected well-developed visuomotor-integrational abilities. No delays were displayed.

Assessment of Brent's academic achievement (i.e., WIAT-III) revealed an achievement profile commensurate with his level of intellect. Abilities of basic reading, reading comprehension, spelling, written expression, and mathematics fell strongly within Average (i.e., normal) range parameters. All results were generally commensurate with his level of intellect.

In sum, Brent's profile is not consistent with any DSM-5 Specific Learning Disorders, including those pertaining to reading and mathematics. There is no indication that Brent demonstrates dyslexia, dysgraphia, or dyscalculia.

Brent's Conners CPT-II profile yielded results that are often consistent with ADHD. Data reflected deficits of visual focused attention, sustained attention, and information processing speed. Results of a competing measure reflected deficits of complex auditory attention and information processing speed. His WISC-IV profile reflected focal weaknesses on tasks examining aspects of working memory and information processing speed.

Neuropsychological test data, clinical interviews, developmental history, clinical observations, and behavior checklists are consistent with a diagnosis (DSM-5) of an Attention-Deficit/Hyperactivity Disorder Predominantly Inattentive Presentation. This ADHD appears to be primarily characterized by symptoms comprising the ADHD symptom cluster of Inattention. Hyperactivity and impulsivity are largely absent.

Brent is a boy who also demonstrates very problematic generalized anxiety. This tendency to worry excessively has reportedly been ongoing since a young age. Psychological exam also indicates the presence of a problematic Generalized Anxiety Disorder (DSM-5). Examination results were not consistent with any competing DSM-5 conditions.

Recommendations: The results of this evaluation were reviewed with Brent and his parents. Education was provided regarding these test results, diagnoses, and treatment options. The following recommendations are offered.

1. I recommend that Brent is linked with a child psychiatrist given his complexity. A referral was sent to Dr. Grenier at the request of Brent's parents. All medication recommendations are deferred to Dr. Grenier. The results of this exam may be helpful in psychiatric treatment planning. At minimum, targeting ADHD via a medication trial would likely be helpful. We will need to closely monitor his response given his concurrent struggles with anxiety. Please discuss medication options with Dr. Grenier in light of the current test results.

2. Behavior modification strategies are important in the management of ADHD. Some examples were discussed and briefly role-played with his parents at the feedback session. A handout outlining a number of specific behavior modification techniques was given to his family. Additional information regarding behavior modification is available via www.chadd.org, www.adhdandyou.com, and my website at www.psychologist.iwarp.com. I recommend that Brent's parents review such information and discuss a specific plan of how they will implement such strategies. Please further discuss the implementation of behavior modification strategies with his therapist.

3. Continue with individual cognitive-behavioral therapy as recommended by his therapist. The results of this exam may be helpful in psychological treatment planning. The following suggestions are also offered.

   Brent could benefit from learning a range of cognitive-behavioral techniques targeting Generalized Anxiety Disorder. For example, he could benefit from structured problem-solving training (e.g., Kendall, Kazdin). He could benefit from learning a range of anxiety management strategies (e.g., diaphragmatic breathing, progressive muscle relaxation training, positive self-talk strategies, visualization, assertiveness training). Teaching him some sleep hygiene techniques and encouraging regular exercise would also be beneficial.

Brent's parents could also probably benefit from a few of their own separate sessions. The focus will be teaching them positive behavior modification strategies to employ at home. I also recommend establishing a home-based contingency management system.

Please discuss with Mr. Beauchamp the development of a psychological treatment plan in light of the current test results.

4. Please bring a copy of this report to Brent's school. Specific accommodations and recommendations are of course deferred to the multidisciplinary team. Results may assist in developing a 504 Plan for Brent given functional academic difficulties stemming from ADHD. The following suggestions may prove helpful.

   1. Provide preferential seating in classroom, near the teacher and away from distracting stimuli.
   2. Repeat directions on an individual basis.
   3. Avoid multiple commands. Give directions in a simple and straightforward manner.
   4. Maintain eye contact with student during verbal directions.
   5. Check student often for understanding of new concepts.
   6. Check to make sure that he wrote down the correct assignment/homework information.
   7. Check to make sure that he handed in necessary assignments and homework.
   8. Provide extra time to complete exams and assignments as necessary.
   9. Develop a communication system with his parents (e.g., e-mail) and use it regularly during the week.
   10. Provide after-school tutoring targeting all areas of academic need.

I appreciate the kind referral and opportunity to provide this evaluation for Brent Mykyte. I will be available for additional consultation as necessary.

Gordon Teichner, PhD, ABPP

Licensed Clinical Psychologist, SC #800

Board Certified in Clinical Psychology, American Board of Professional Psychology

About the Author

Gordon Teichner, PhD, ABPP, is a Neuropsychologist/Clinical Psychologist who has an individual private practice in Charleston, South Carolina. He has over 20 years of experience evaluating and treating children and adolescents who demonstrate an Attention-Deficit/Hyperactivity Disorder. Dr. Teichner completed a PhD in Clinical Psychology, with a specialty in Neuropsychology, from Nova Southeastern University. He completed his Clinical Psychology Internship, which included a 50 percent Neuropsychology emphasis, at the Medical University of South Carolina/Ralph H. Johnson Department of Veterans Affairs Medical Center Consortium in Charleston, South Carolina. He then completed a two-year Neuropsychology Fellowship at the Medical University of South Carolina. Dr. Teichner is Board Certified in Clinical Psychology by the American Board of Professional Psychology. He is a Fellow of the American Academy of Clinical Psychology. Dr. Teichner has conducted extensive research. He has been an investigator in multiple studies examining the efficacy of different medication for ADHD in children, adolescents, and adults. He has authored or coauthored 26 scientific articles in peer-reviewed journals and 23 journal abstracts, and has given 80+ presentations (posters, papers, and symposia) at national and state conferences of prominent organizations, including the National Academy of Neuropsychology, International Neuropsychological Society, American Psychological Association, and the American Academy of Behavior Therapy. Dr. Teichner is a member of the National Academy of Neuropsychology, American Psychological Association, American Psychological Association Division 40 (Neuropsychology), South Carolina Psychological Association, American Board of Professional Psychology, and American Academy of Clinical Psychology.

Bibliography

Achenbach, T. M. (2009). *The Achenbach System of Empirically Based Assessment (ASEBA): Development, Findings, Theory, and Applications.* Burlington, VT: University of Vermont Research Center for Children, Youth, & Families.

Achenbach, T. M., & Rescorla, L. A. (2000). *Manual for the ASEBA Preschool Forms & Profiles.* Burlington, VT: University of Vermont, Research Center for Children, Youth, & Families.

Achenbach, T. M., & Rescorla, L. A. (2001). *Manual for the ASEBA School-Age Forms & Profiles.* Burlington, VT: University of Vermont, Research Center for Children, Youth, & Families.

Achenbach, T. M., & Ruffle, T. M. (2000). The Child Behavior Checklist and related forms for assessing behavioral/emotional problems and competencies. *Pediatr Rev,* 21(8), 265–271.

Achenbach, T. M., Rescorla, L. A., & Ivanova, M. Y. (2012). International epidemiology of child and adolescent psychopathology I: diagnoses, dimensions, and conceptual issues. *Journal of the American Academy of Child Adolescent Psychiatry,* 51(12), 1261–1272.

Alfano, K., & Boone, K. (2007). The use of effort tests in context of actual versus feigned attention deficit hyperactivity disorder/learning disability. In K. Boone (ed.), *Assessment of Feigned Cognitive Impairment* (pp. 366–383). New York, NY: Guilford Press.

American Psychiatric Association (1994). Diagnostic and Statistical Manual of Mental Disorders: Fourth Edition. American Psychiatric Association. Washington, DC.

American Psychiatric Association (2000). Diagnostic and Statistical Manual of Mental Disorders: Fourth Edition—TR. American Psychiatric Association. Washington, DC.

American Psychiatric Association (2013). Diagnostic and Statistical Manual of Mental Disorders: Fifth Edition. American Psychiatric Association. Arlington, VA.

American Psychological Association (2011). Practice guidelines regarding psychologists involvement in pharmacological issues. *American psychologist,* 66(9), 838–839. doi:10.1037/a0025890

Bader, A., & Adesman, A. (2015). Complementary and alternative medicine for ADHD. In R. A. Barkley (ed.), *Attention-Deficit Hyperactivity Disorder* (4th ed., pp. 728–738). New York, NY: The Guildford Press.

Bard, D. E., Wolraich, M. L., Neas, B., Doffing, M., & Beck, L. (2013). The psychometric properties of the vanderbilt attention-deficit hyperactivity disorder diagnostic parent rating scale in a community population. *Journal of Developmental Behavioral Pediatrics*, 34, 72–82.

Barkley, R. A. (2000). ADHD, Part I: The executive functions and ADHD. *Journal Am Acad Child Adolescent Psychiatry*, 39(8), 1064–1068.

Barkley, R. A. (2012). *Barkley Deficits in Executive Functioning Scale: Children & Adolescents (BDEFS-CA)*. New York, NY: The Guilford Press.

Barkley, R. A. (2012). *Barkley Deficits in Executive Functioning Scale—Child & Adolescent*. New York, NY: The Guildford Press.

Barkley, R. A. (2015). Etiologies of ADHD. In R. A. Barkley (ed.), *Attention-Deficit Hyperactivity Disorder* (4th ed., pp. 356–390). New York, NY: The Guildford Press.

Barkley, R. A., & Robin, A. L. (2014). *Defiant teens: A clinician's manual for assessment and family intervention*. 2nd ed. New York: Guilford Press.

Barkley, R. A., Cook, E. H., Diamond, A., Zametkin, A., Thapar, A., & Teeter, A. (2002). International consensus statement on ADHD. *Clinical Child and Family Psychology Review*, 5(2), 89–111.

Barkley, R. A. (2013). *Defiant children: A clinician's manual for assessment and parent training*. 3rd ed. New York: Guilford Press.

Barkley, R. A., & Murphy, K. R. (1998). Attention-Deficit/Hyperactivity Disorder: A clinical workbook. 2nd ed. New York, NY: The Guildford Press.

Barkley, R. A., & Murphy, K. R. (2006). Attention-Deficit/Hyperactivity Disorder: A clinical workbook. 3rd ed. New York, NY: The Guildford Press.

Beery, K. E., Buktenica, N. A., & Beery, N. A. (2010). *Beery-Buktenica developmental test of visual-perception*. 6th ed. Bloomington, MN: Pearson.

Benton, A. L., Sivan, A. B., Hamsher, K., Varney, N. R., & Spreen, O. (1994). Contributions to neuropsychological assessment—A clinical manual. Lutz, FL: Psychological Assessment Resources.

Bracken, B. A., & Keith, K. L. (2004). CAB—Clinical assessment of behavior. Lutz, FL: Psychological Assessment Resources.

Brown, T. E. (1996). *Brown attention-deficit disorder scales*. San Antonio, TX: The Psychological Corporation.

Brown, T. E. (2001). *Brown attention-deficit disorder scales for children and adolescents*. Bloomington, MN: NCS Pearson.

Brown, T. E. (2006). Executive functions and attention deficit hyperactivity disorder: Implications of two conflicting views. *International Journal of Disability, Development and Education*, 53(1), 35–46.

Centers for Disease Control (1991). *Preventing lead poisoning in young children: a statement by the Centers for Disease Control*. Atlanta, GA: US Department of Health and Human Services.

Centers for Disease Control (2012). *Healthy homes and lead poisoning prevention: what do parents need to know to protect their children?* Atlanta, GA: US Department of Health and Human Services.

Chacko, A., Allan, C. C., Uderman, J., Cornwell, M., Anderson, L., & Chimiklis, A. (2015). Training parents of youth with ADHD. In R. A. Barkley (ed.), *Attention-Deficit Hyperactivity Disorder* (4th ed., pp. 513–536). New York, NY: The Guildford Press.

Chan, E., Fogler, J. M., Hammerness, P. G. (2016). Treatment of Attention-Deficit/Hyperactivity Disorder in Adolescents: A Systematic Review. *JAMA*, 315(18), 1997–2008. doi:10.1001/jama.2016.5453.

Coates, J., Taylor, J. A., Sayal, K. (2014). Parenting interventions for ADHD: A systematic literature review and meta-analysis. *Journal of Attention Disorders*, epub. doi:10.1177/1087054714535952

Cohen, J. (1988). *Statistical power analysis for the behavioral sciences.* 2nd ed. Hillsdale, NJ: Erlbaum.

Cohen, M. J. (1997). *Children's memory scale.* San Antonio, TX: The Psychological Corporation.

Conners, C. K. (1969). A teacher rating scale for use in drug studies with children. *American Journal of Psychiatry*, 126, 884–888.

Conners, C. K. (2004). *Conners continuous performance test—II version 5 for windows (CPT II V.5).* North Tonawanda, NY: Multihealth Systems, Inc.

Conners, C. K. (2008). *Manual for the Conners 3.* North Tonawanda, NY: Multi-Health Systems.

Conners, C. K. (2014). *Conners continuous auditory test of attention (Conners CATA).* North Tonawanda, NY: Multihealth Systems, Inc.

Conners, C. K. (2014). *Conners continuous performance test.* 3rd ed (CPT 3). North Tonawanda, NY: Multihealth Systems, Inc.

Cortese, S., Ferrin, M., Brandeis, D., Holtmann, M., Aggensteiner, P., Daley, D., Santosh, P., Simonoff, E., Stevenson, J., Stringaris, A., Sonuga-Barke, E. J. S., on behalf of the European ADHD Guidelines Group (EAGG), Asherson, P., Banaschewski, T., Brandeis, D., Buitelaar, J., Coghill, D., Cortese, S., Daley, D., Danckaerts, M., Dittmann, R. W., Döpfner, M., Ferrin, M., Hollis, C., Holtmann, M., Konofal, E., Lecendreux, M., Rothenberger, A., Santosh, P., Sergeant, J. A., Simonoff, E., Sonuga-Barke, E. J., Soutullo, C., Steinhausen, H. C., Stevenson, J., Stringaris, A., Taylor, E., van der Oord, S., Wong, I., Zuddas, A. (2016). Neurofeedback for attention-deficit/hyperactivity disorder: Meta-analysis of clinical and neuropsychological outcomes from randomized controlled trials. *Journal of the American Academy of Child & Adolescent Psychiatry.* doi:10.1016/j.jaac.2016.03.007

Cunningham, C. E., Bremner, R.B., Secord-Gilbert, M. (1998). *COPE: The community parent education program: A school-based family systems oriented workshop for parents of children with disruptive behavior disorders.* Hamilton, Ontario: COPE Works.

Dean, R. S., & Woodcock, R. W. (2003). *Dean-Woodcock Neuropsychological Battery.* Itasca, IL: Riverside Publishing.

Delis, D. (2012). *Delis rating of executive function (D-REF).* Bloomington, MN: Pearson.

Delis, D. C., Kaplan, E., & Kramer, J. H. (2001). Delis-Kaplin executive function system. San Antonio, TX: The Psychological Corporation.

Delis, D. C., Kramer, J. H., Kaplan, E., & Ober, B. A. (1994). *California verbal learning test-children's version.* San Antonio, TX: The Psychological Corporation.

Diehr, M. C., Heaton, R. K., Miller, W., & Grant, W. (1998). The Paced Auditory Serial Addition Test (PASAT): Norms for age, education and ethnicity. *Assessment,* 5(4), 375–387.

DuPaul, G. J., & Stoner, G. (2014). *ADHD in the schools: Assessment and intervention strategies.* 3rd ed. New York: Guilford Press.

DuPaul, G. J., Gormley, M. J., & Laracy, S. D. (2013). Comorbidity of LD and ADHD: Implications of DSM-5 for assessment and treatment. *Journal of Learning Disabilities,* 46(1), 43–51.

DuPaul, G. J., Power, T. J., Anastopoulos, A. D., & Reid, R. (1998). *ADHD Rating Scale—IV: Checklists, norms, and clinical interpretation.* New York: Guilford Press.

Elliott, C. D. (2006). *Differential ability scales—Second Edition (DAS-II).* San Antonio, TX: Psychological Corporation.

Eriksson, M., Jonsson, B., Steneroth, G., & Zetterstrom, R. (2000). Amphetamine abuse during pregnancy: environmental factors and outcome after 14–15 years. *Scandinavian Journal of Public Health,* 28, 154–157.

Faraone, S. V. (2009). Using Meta-analysis to compare the efficacy of medications for Attention-Deficit/Hyperactivity Disorder in youths. *Pharmacy & Therapeutics,* 34(12), 678–683.

Faraone, S. V., Biederman, J., Morley, C. P., & Spencer, T. J. (2008). Effect of stimulants on height and weight: A review of the literature. *Journal of the American Academy of Child and Adolescent Psychiatry,* 47(9), 994–1009.

Faraone, S. V., Perlis, R. H., Doyle, A. E., Smoller, J. W., Goralnick, J. J., Holmgren, M. A., & Sklar, P. (2005). Molecular genetics of attention-deficit/ hyperactivity disorder. *Biological Psychiatry,* 57, 1313–1323.

Figueroa, R. M. D. P. (2010). Use of antidepressants during pregnancy and risk of Attention-Deficit / Hyperactivity disorder in the offspring. *Journal of Developmental Behavioral Pediatrics,* 31, 641–648.

Frederick, R. I. (2003). *The validity indicator profile.* 2nd ed. Minnesota, MN: NCS Pearson.

Froehlich, T. E., Anixt, J. S., Loe, I. M., Chirdkiatgumchai, V., Kuan, L., & Gilman, R. C. (2011). Update on environmental risk factors for attention-deficit/hyperactivity disorder. *Current Psychiatry Reports*, 13(5), 333–344.

Gaastra, G. F., Groen, Y., Tucha, L., & Tucha, O. (2016). The effects of classroom interventions on off-task and disruptive classroom behavior in children with symptoms of Attention-Deficit/Hyperactivity Disorder: A Meta-Analytic Review. *PloS One*, 11(2), 1–19, e0148841. doi:10.1371/journal.pone.0148841

Gardner, R. A., & Broman, M. (1979). The purdue pegboard: Normative data on 1334 school children. *Journal of Clinical Child Psychology*, 8, 156–162.

Gioia, G. A., Isquith, P. K., Guy, S. C., & Kenworthy, L. (2015). *Behavior rating inventory of executive function - Second Edition (BRIEF-2)*. Odessa, FL: Psychological Assessment Resources.

Golden, C. J., & Freshwater, S. M. (2002). *Stroop color and word test: Revised examiner's manual*. Wood Date, IL: Stoelting Co.

Golden, C. J., Freshwater, S. M., & Golden, Z. (2003). *Stroop color and word test children's version for ages 5–14*. Wood Date, IL: Stoelting Co.

Goodlad, J. K., Marcus, D. K., & Fulton, J. J. (2013). Lead and attention-deficit/hyperactivty disorder (ADHD) symptoms: A meta analysis. *Clinical Psychology Review*, 33, 417–425.

Green, P. (2003). *Word memory test for windows: User's manual and program*. Edmonton: Green's Publishing.

Green, P. (2004). Medical symptom validity test for windows: User's manual and program. Edmonton: Green's Publishing.

Gronwall, D. M. (1977). Paced auditory serial addition task: A measure of recovery from concussion. *Perceptual and Motor Skills*, 44, 367–373.

Ha, M., Kwon, H. J., Lim, M. H., Lee, Y. K., Hong, Y. C., Leem, J. H., et al. (2009). Low blood levels of lead and mercury and symptoms of Attention-Deficit / Hyperactivity Disorder in children: A report of the Children's Health and Environment Research (CHEER). *Neurotoxicology*, 30, 31–36.

Hammill, D. D., & Newcomer, P. L. (2008). *Test of Language Development–Intermediate: 4th Ed. (TOLD-I:4)*. Austin, TX: Pro-Ed.

Heaton, R. K., Chelune, G. J., Talley, J. L., Kay, G. G., & Curtis, G. (1993). *Wisconsin Card Sorting Test (WCST) manual, revised and expanded*. Odessa, FL: Psychological Assessment Resources.

Hinshaw, S. P., Owens, E. B., Zalecki, C., Huggins, S. P., Montenegro-Nevado, A., Schrodek, E., & Swanson, E. N. (2012). Prospective follow-up of girls with attention-deficit hyperactivity disorder into early adulthood. Continuing impairment includes elevated risk for suicide attempts and self-injury. *Journal of Consulting and Clinical Psychology*, 80(6), 1041–1051.

Hodges, K., McKnew, D., Cytryn, L., Stern, L., & Kline, J. (1982). The Child Assessment Schedule (CAS) diagnostic interview: A report on reliability and validity. *Journal of the American Academy of Child Psychiatry*, 21, 468–473.

Johnson, D. A., Roethig-Johnson, K., & Middleton, J. (1988). Development and evaluation of an attentional test for head-injured children: 1. Information processing capacity in a normal sample. *Journal of Child Psychology and Psychiatry*, 2, 199–208.

Kaufman J., Birmaher, B., Brent, D., Rao, U., Ryan, N. (1996). *Kiddie-SADS-Present and Lifetime Version (K-SADS-PL), Version 1.0*. Pittsburgh: Department of Psychiatry, University of Pittsburgh School of Medicine.

Kaufman, A. S., & Kaufman, N. L. (2004). *Kaufman Assessment Battery for Children - II (KABC-II)*. Circle Press, MN: American Guidance Service.

Kaufman, A. S., & Kaufman, N. L. (2014). *Kaufman test of educational achievement, Third Edition (KTEA-3)*. Bloomington, MN: Pearson.

Kazdin, A. (2005). *Parent management training: Treatment for oppositional, aggressive, and antisocial behavior in children and adolescents*. New York: Oxford University Press.

Korkman, M., Kirk, U., & Kemp, S. (2007). *NEPSY-II: A developmental neuropsychological assessment*. San Antonio, TX: The Psychological Corporation.

Leark, R. A., Greenberg, L. K., Kindschi, C. L., Dupuy, T. R., & Hughes, S. J. (2007). *Test of Variables of Attention: Professional Manual*. Los Alamitos: The TOVA Company.

Llorente, A. M., Williams, J., Satz, P., & D'Elia, L. (2003). *Children's Color Trails Test (CCTT)*. Odessa, FL: Psychological Assessment Resources.

Loney, J., & Milich, R. (1982). Hyperactivity, inattention, and aggression in clinical practice. In M. Wolraich & D. K. Routh (eds.), *Advances in developmental and behavioral pediatrics* (Vol. 3, pp. 113–147). Greenwich, CT: JAI.

Manly, T., Robertson, I. H., Anderson, V., & Nimmo-Smith, I. (1999). *TEA-Ch: The test of everyday attention for children*. Bury St., Edmunds, UK: Thames Valley Test Company.

Martin, N. (2006). Test of visual-perception skills - 3rd Edition. Navato, CA: Academic Therapy Publications.

Martin, N., & Brownell, R. (2005). *Test of auditory processing skills-3*. Novato, CA: Academic Therapy Publications.

Matthews, C. G., & Klove, K. (1964). *Instruction manual for the Adult Neuropsychology Test Battery*. Madison, Wisc.: University of Wisconsin Medical School.

McNeil, C. B., & Hembree-Kigin, T. L. (2010). *Parent-child interaction therapy*. 2nd ed. New York: Springer.

Meyers, J. E., & Meyers, K. R. (1995). *Rey complex figure test and recognition trial.* Odessa, FL: Psychological Assessment Resources.

Mick, E., Biederman, J., Faraone, S. V., Sayer, J., & Kleinman, S. (2002). Case-control study of attention-deficit hyperactivity disorder and maternal smoking, alcohol use, and drug use during pregnancy. *Journal of the American Academy of Child and Adolescent Psychiatry,* 41, 378–385.

Morrow, C. E., Accornero, V. H., Xue, L., Manjunath, S., Culbertson, J. L., Anthony, J. C., & Bandstra, E. S. (2009). Estimated risk of developing selected DSM-IV disorders among 5-year-old children with prenatal cocaine exposure. *Journal of Child and family Studies,* 18, 356–364.

MTA Cooperative Group (1999). A 14-month randomized clinical trial of treatment strategies for Attention-Deficit/Hyperactivity Disorder: The MTA Cooperative Group Multimodal Treatment Study of children with ADHD. *Archives of General Psychiatry,* 56(12), 1073–1086.

Murray, M. J. (2010). Attention-deficit/hyperactivity disorder in the context of autism spectrum disorders. *Current Psychiatric Reports,* 12(5), 382–388.

Nicholas, P. L., & Chen, T. C. (1981). *Minimal brain dysfunction: A prospective study.* Hillsdale, NJ: Erlbaum.

Nigg, J. T., Knottnerus, G. M., Martel, M. N., Nikolas, M., Cavanagh, K., Karmaus, W., & Rappley, M. D. (2008). Low blood lead levels associated with clinically diagnosed attention-deficit/hyperactivity disorder and mediated by weak cognitive control. *Biological Psychiatry,* 63(3), 325–331.

Nigg, J. T., Nikolas, M., Knottnerus, G. M., Cavanagh, K., & Friderici, K. (2010). Confirmation and extension of association of blood lead with attention-deficit/hyperactivity disorder (ADHD) and ADHD symptom domains at population—typical exposure levels. *Journal of Child Psychology & Psychiatry,* 51(1), 58–65.

Nikolas, M. A., & Burt, S. A. (2010). Genetic and environmental influences on ADHD symptom dimensions of inattention and hyperactivity: A meta-analysis. *Journal of Abnormal Psychology,* 119, 1–17.

Nulman, I., Rovet, J., Stewart, D. E., Wolpin, J., Pace-Asciak, P., Shuhaiber, S., & Koren, G. (2002). Child development following exposure to tricyclic antidepressants or fluoxetine throughout fetal life: a prospective, controlled study. *American Journal of Psychiatry,* 159(11), 1889–1895.

Oberlander, T. F., Reebye, P., Misri, S., Papsdorf, M., Kim, J., & Grunau, R. E. (2007). Externalizing and attentional behaviors in children of depressed mothers treated with a selective serotonin reuptake inhibitor antidepressant during pregnancy. *Archives of Pediatric Adolescent Medicine,* 161(1), 22–29.

Ornoy, A., Michailevskaya, V., Lukashov, I., Bar-Hamburger, R., & Harel, S. (1996). The developmental outcome of children born to heroin-dependent mothers, raised at home or adopted. *Child Abuse & Neglect,* 20, 385–396.

Pfiffner, L. J., & DuPaul, G. J. (2015). Treatment of ADHD in school settings. In R. A. Barkley (ed.), *Attention-Deficit Hyperactivity Disorder* (4th ed., pp. 596–629). New York, NY: The Guilford Press.

Pliszka, S. (2007). Practice parameter for the assessment and treatment of children and adolescents with attention-deficit/hyperactivity disorder. *Journal of the American Academy of Child and Adolescent Psychiatry*, 46(7), 894–921.

Polanska, K., Jurewicz, J., & Hanke, W. (2013). Review of current evidence on the impact of pesticides, polychlorinated biphenyls and selected metals on attention deficit / hyperactivity disorder in children. *International Journal of Occupational Medicine and Environmental Health*, 26, 16–38.

Raymond, J., & Brown, M. J. (2016). Blood lead levels in children aged <5 Years—United States, 2007–2013. *Centers for Disease Control and Prevention (CDC)—Morbidity and Mortality Weekly Report*, 63(55), 66–72.

Reich, W., Welner, Z., Herjanic, B., & MHS staff. (1996). *Diagnostic interview for children and adolescents-IV computer program (DICA-IV)*. New York: Multihealth Systems.

Reitan, R. M. (1955). The relation of the Trail Making Test to organic brain damage. *Journal of Consulting Psychology*, 19, 393–394.

Reitan, R. M. (1969). *Manual for the administration of neuropsychological test batteries for adults and children*. Indianapolis, Indiana.

Reitan, R. M., & Wolfson, D. (2004). Trail Making Test as an initial screening procedure for neuropsychological impairment in older children. *Archives of Clinical Neuropsychology*, 19, 281–288.

Reynolds, C. R. (2002). *Comprehensive Trail Making Test*. Odessa, FL: Psychological Assessment Resources.

Reynolds, C. R., & Kamphaus, R. W. (1992). *BASC: Behavior assessment system for children: Manual*. American Guidance Service, Incorporated.

Reynolds, C. R., & Kamphaus, R. W. (2004). *Behavior assessment system for children—Second edition*. Bloomington, MN: Pearson.

Reynolds, C. R., & Kamphaus, R. W. (2015). *Behavior assessment system for children—Third Edition*. Bloomington, MN: Pearson.

Reynolds, C. R., & Kamphaus, R. W. (2015). *Reynolds intellectual assessment scales, second ed. and the Reynolds intellectual screening test*. 2nd ed. Lutz, FL: PAR.

Reynolds, C. R., & Voress, J. K. (2007). *Test of Memory and Learning - Second Edition*. Austin, TX: PRO-ED.

Reynolds, W. M. (1998). *Adolescent psychopathology scale*. Odessa, FL, Psychological Assessment Resources.

Robin, A. L. (2015). Training Families of Adolescents with ADHD. In R. A. Barkley (ed.), *Attention-Deficit Hyperactivity Disorder* (4th ed., pp. 537–568). New York, NY: The Guildford Press.

Roid, G. H. (2003). *Stanford-Binet intelligence scales: Fifth Edition.* Itasca, IL: Riverside.

Rothenberger, A., Roessner, V., Banaschewski, T., & Leckman, J. F. (2007). Co-existence of tic disorders and Attention-Deficit/Hyperactivity Disorder: Recent advances in understanding and treatment. *European Child and Adolescent Psychiatry,* 16(Suppl. 1), 1–4.

Sandford, J. A., & Turner, A. (2004). *Manual for the integrated visual and auditory continuous performance test.* Richmond, VA: Brain Train.

Schothorst, P. F., & van Engeland, H. (1996). Long-term behavioral sequelae of prematurity. *Journal of the American Academy of Child and Adolescent Psychiatry,* 35, 175–183.

Schrank, F. A., Mather, N., & McGrew, K. S. (2014). *Woodcock-Johnson IV Tests of Achievement.* Rolling Meadows, IL: Riverside.

Schrank, F. A., McGrew, K. S., & Mather, N. (2014). *Woodcock-Johnson IV Tests of Cognitive Abilities.* Rolling Meadows, IL: Riverside.

Schretlen, D. (1997). *Brief Test of Attention professional manual.* Odessa, FL: Psychological Assessment Resources.

Shaffer, D., Fisher, P., & Lucas, C. P., Dulcan, M. K., & Schwab-Stone, M. E. (2000). NIMH Diagnostic Interview Schedule for children version IV (NIMH DISC-IV): Description, differences from previous versions, and reliability of some common diagnoses. *Journal of the American Academy of Child & Adolescent Psychiatry,* 39, 28–38.

Sheehan, D., Sheehan, K., Shytle, R., Janavs, J., Bannon, Y., Rogers, J., Milo, K., Stock, S., & Wilkinson, B. (2010). Reliability and validity of the Mini International Neuropsychiatric Interview for Children and Adolescents (MINI-KID). *Journal of Clinical Psychiatry,* 71(3), 313–326. doi:10.4088/JCP.09m05305whi

Sheslow, D., & Adams, W. (2003). Wide range assessment of memory and learning. 2nd ed. Wilmington, Delaware: Wide Range.

Sonuga-Barke, E. J., Brandeis, D., Cortese, S., Daley, D., Ferrin, M., Holtmann, M., Stevenson, J., Danckaerts, M., Van der Oord, S., Döpfner, M., & Dittmann, R. W. (2013). Nonpharmacological interventions for ADHD: systematic review and meta-analyses of randomized controlled trials of dietary and psychological treatments. *American Journal of Psychiatry,* 170(3), 275–289.

Stroop, J. R. (1935). Studies of interference in serial verbal reaction. *Journal of Experimental Psychology,* 18, 643–662.

Suhr, J., Hammers, D., Dobbins-Buckland, K., Zimak, E., & Hughes, C. (2008). The relationship of malingering test failure to self-reported symptoms and neuropsychological findings in adults referred for ADHD evaluation. *Archives of Clinical Neuropsychology,* 23, 521–530. doi:10.1016/j.acn.2008.05.003

Sullivan, B. K., May, K., & Galbally, L. (2007). Symptom exaggeration by college adults in Attention-Deficit Hyperactivity Disorder and Learning Disorder Assessments. *Applied Neuropsychology*, 14(3), 189–207. http://dx.doi.org/10.1080/09084280701509083.

Swanson, J. M., Sandman, C. A., Deutsch, C., & Baren, M. (1983). Methylphenidate hydrochloride given with or before breakfast: I. Behavioral, cognitive, and electrophysiologic effects. *Pediatrics*, 72, 49–55.

Swanson, J. M., Wigal, S., Greenhill, L. L., Browne, R., Waslik, B., Lerner, M., Williams, L., Flynn, D., Agler, D., Crowley, K., Fineberg, E., Baren, M., & Cantwell, D. P. (1998). Analog classroom assessment of Adderall in children with ADHD. *J Am Acad Child Adolesc Psychiatry*, 37, 519–526.

Tanaka, Y., Rohde, L. A., Jin, L., Feldman, P. D., & Upadhyaya, H. P. (2013). A meta-analysis of the consistency of atomoxetine treatment effects in pediatric patients with Attention-Deficit / Hyperactivity Disorder from 15 clinical trials across four geographic regions. *Journal of Child and Adolescent Psychopharmacology*, 23(4), 262–270.

Thapar, A., Cooper, M., Eyre, O., & Langley, K. (2013). What have we learnt about the causes of ADHD? *Journal of Child Psychology and Psychiatry, and Allied Disciplines*, 54(1), 3–16.

Tombaugh, T. N. (1996). *Test of Memory Malingering (TOMM)*. New York: Multi-Health Systems, Inc.

Wagner, R., Torgesen, J., Rashotte, C., & Pearson, N. A. (2013). *Comprehensive Test of Phonological Processing, Second Edition (CTOPP-2)*. Bloomington, MN: Pearson.

Wechsler, D. (2008). *The Wechsler adult intelligence scale*. 4th ed. Bloomington, MN: Pearson.

Wechsler, D. (2009). *Wechsler individual achievement test*. 3rd ed. Bloomington, MN: Pearson.

Wechsler, D. (2011). The Wechsler abbreviated scale of intelligence. 2nd ed. Bloomington, MN: Pearson.

Wechsler, D. (2012). Wechsler preschool and primary scale of intelligence. 4th ed. Bloomington, MN: Pearson.

Wechsler, D. (2014). The Wechsler intelligence scale for children. 5th ed. Bloomington, MN: Pearson.

Wiederholt, J. L., & Bryant, B. R. (2012). *Gray Oral Reading Tests - Fifth Edition (GORT-5)*. Austin, TX: PRO-ED.

Wiig, E. H., Semel, E., & Secord, W. A. (2013). *Clinical Evaluation of Language Fundamentals—Fifth Edition (CELF-5)*. Bloomington, MN: Pearson.

Wilens, T. E., Robertson, B., Sikerica V., et al. (2015). A randomized, placebo-controlled trial of guanfacine-extended release in adolescents with attention-deficit/hyperactivity disorder. *Journal of the American Academy of Child and Adolescent Psychiatry*, 54(11), 916–925.

Wilkinson, G. S., & Robertson, G. J. (2006). *Wide Range Achievement Test 4.* Lutz, FL: Psychological Assessment Resources.

Willcutt, E. G., & Bidwell, C. (2011). Neuropsychology of attention deficit hyperactivity disorder: Implications for assessment and treatment. In S. E. Evans & B. Hoza (eds.), *Treating attention deficit hyperactivity disorder: Assessment and intervention in developmental context* (pp. 6.2–6.24). Kingston, NJ: Civic Research Institute.

Williams, J. H., & Ross, L. (2007). Consequences of prenatal toxin exposure for mental health in children and adolescents: a systematic review. *European Child & Adolescent Psychiatry*, 16, 243–253.

Wolraich, M. L., Feurer, I. D., Hannah, J. N., Pinnock, T.Y., & Baumgartner, A. (1998). Obtaining systematic teacher reports of disruptive behavior disorders utilizing DSM-IV. *Journal of Abnormal Child Psychology*, 26(2), 141–152.

Wolraich, M. L., Lambert, W., Simmons, T., Worley, K., Doffing, M. A., & Bickman, L. (2003). Psychometric properties of the vanderbilt ADHD diagnostic parent rating scale in a referred population. *Journal of Pediatric Psychology*, 28(8), 559–568.

Yang, L., Neale, B. M., Liu, L., Lee, S. H., Wray, N. R., Ji, N., Li, H., Qian, Q., Wang, D., Li, J., & Faraone, S. V. (2013). Polygenetic transmission and complex neurodevelopmental network for attention deficit hyperactivity disorder: Genome-wide association study of both common and rare variants. *American Journal of Medical Genetics B: Neuropsychiatric Genetics*, 162, 419–430.

Young, S. (2015). ADHD Child Evaluation (ACE). A diagnostic interview of ADHD in children. Psychology Services Limited.

Index

OTHER TITLES IN THIS CHILD CLINICAL PSYCHOLOGY "NUTS AND BOLTS" COLLECTION

Samuel T. Gontkovsky, *Editor*

Childhood Anxiety Disorders
by Ashley J. Smith and Amy M. Jacobson

*Posttraumatic Stress Disorder in Childhood and Adolescence:
A Developmental Psychopathology Perspective*
by Patricia K. Kerig

Disruptive Behavior Disorders in Children
by Meredith Weber and Erica Burgoon

Pediatric Bipolar Spectrum Disorder
by Elizabeth B. Hamilton, Kristie Knows His Gun,
and Christina W. Tuning

Momentum Press is one of the leading book publishers in the field of engineering, mathematics, health, and applied sciences. Momentum Press offers over 30 collections, including Aerospace, Biomedical, Civil, Environmental, Nanomaterials, Geotechnical, and many others.

Momentum Press is actively seeking collection editors as well as authors. For more information about becoming an MP author or collection editor, please visit http://www.momentumpress.net/contact

---

Announcing Digital Content Crafted by Librarians

Momentum Press offers digital content as authoritative treatments of advanced engineering topics by leaders in their field. Hosted on ebrary, MP provides practitioners, researchers, faculty, and students in engineering, science, and industry with innovative electronic content in sensors and controls engineering, advanced energy engineering, manufacturing, and materials science.

Momentum Press offers library-friendly terms:

- perpetual access for a one-time fee
- no subscriptions or access fees required
- unlimited concurrent usage permitted
- downloadable PDFs provided
- free MARC records included
- free trials

The **Momentum Press** digital library is very affordable, with no obligation to buy in future years.

For more information, please visit **www.momentumpress.net/library** or to set up a trial in the US, please contact **mpsales@globalepress.com**.

www.ingramcontent.com/pod-product-compliance
Lightning Source LLC
Chambersburg PA
CBHW050716280326
41926CB00088B/3063